TESTIMONIALS FROM AROUND THE WORLD

In the mid-1980s to early 1990s, Msaada was invaluable to me in two major construction projects. I cannot say enough good things about the Arusha staff over the years, both expatriate and local, always with the backup presence of the home office.
~**Rev. Gerry Kohler**, CCSp, Roman Catholic former missionary priest in Tanzania

The building looks great. It is coming together very well. I can't thank you enough for your work here. I am also glad you have been able to hold the line on the budget. It not only gives you credibility but also our field staff when we ask for more money to build.
~**Rev. Dr. Brent Smith**, LCMS World Mission Regional Director for Eurasia.

The church building has come up very nicely, and every detail is being studied. It stands very beautifully, and I can't find words to describe it. In the nights, with all the lights on, it is simply beautiful. Whenever we sit for prayers in the beautiful church, Msaada's name will be remembered. And the more we use the church, the more beautiful it seems to become.
~**Ms. Prabha Joseph**, former Managing Director of Sevamandir Girls' Boarding School in India

As a young architect with a few years' experience in commercial and residential practice, I had already decided to abandon my chosen profession to explore a career in linguistics owing to my disappointment with a profession that I found to be self-serving and only marginally concerned with matters of real importance to people's lives. The life-changing experience of serving through Msaada has defined me as a person and as an architect and still informs my work today as a professor of architecture.
~**Peter Ozolins**, former employee, and resident architect of Madagascar area office and later professor of architecture

We are so pleased that you were able to teach and hope you are interested in doing so again. Thank you for sharing your experience so generously.

~**Renee Cheng**, former head of the School of Architecture in the College of Design at the University of Minnesota, after Poul Bertelsen had become part-time "Professor in Practice".

This time it was again almost 'scary' how much went according to what had been planned...or even better! Therefore, maybe the situation is that there was nothing specific to point out? Instead, the whole project has been moving along in its own quiet and efficient way, with a lot of local involvement, but also without a lot of 'drama.' Parallel with that, it carefully has followed the laid-out plans and ideas for the objectives to be met...[this] is, in fact, the true story behind the project...and that is not a small accomplishment!
~**The Danish Government's Aid Organization** (DANIDA) re a large School Project in India

The new hospital is an impressive structure, which is in harmony with its surrounding terrain. The many different departments witness to Msaada's careful planning and design work. Thus, the whole hospital complex presents itself as a very functional 110-bed facility. We got a lot of value for the money spent on this project!
~**Local Lutheran Church** as owner plus the funders of a new Bunda Hospital in Tanzania

I want to thank you again for the beautiful ICRC building. I was told by the ICRC that you did a terrific job throughout the entire project, that your plans were superlative and that they would highly recommend you. I was extremely impressed with the building when I finally got to see it at the opening ceremony.
~**Dr. Steve Fisher**, former Board Chair of Healing Hands for Haiti

Saron has in recent years got some new buildings that have entirely changed the appearance of that old mission station. Earlier, it was mostly an old beautiful bungalow, maybe the most beautiful in the area, with some low school buildings and the church. But now everything has, through the additions of some large modern buildings, been joined together in a complex that is without its equal in beauty and harmony. It is a joy to see how new structures blend with old. And trees that were on site have been kept, and some existing rock formations have become part of an attractive rock garden.
~**Rt. Rev. Thorkild Graesholt**, former Chair of Danish Mission Society (now Danmission)

The church in Vadalur, which was built in Indian style and inaugurated in 1988, is in constant dialogue with people of other faiths... This structure with architectural detailing of the broader religious India, is a "signboard" for the Arcot Lutheran Church. It invites discussions inside and outside the church about the necessity for dialogue and content in evangelism in the midst of the multi-religious Indian sub-continent.
~**Rt. Rev. Raja Socrates**, former Bishop of Arcot Lutheran Church in Tamil Nadu, India

Though I know I am no longer officially a part of the Msaada team, I find myself talking about the work, the mission, and the projects almost daily. Being a part of the Msaada Team was and is a big part of my identity.
~**Jason Krumm**, former staff architect

As I drove home, however, your words echoed in my mind: 'Never lose your enthusiasm and idealism.' And I then realized that no matter how much time I will spend learning architecture theory, I will always adhere to what I learned at Msaada: that good design and quality construction don't need to be expensive. That it's important to design culturally and geographically appropriate structures. And, most importantly, that architecture above else, is about serving others — in particular others who have so much less than we have financially.
~**Erica Boyles**, commencing studying architecture, after she had done clerical work for Msaada.

The Malagasy Lutheran Church Health Department (SALFA) accomplished many building projects with Msaada's invaluable assistance, which kept us from overstepping our budgetary restraints, kept us in line with standards of building construction, allowed us to negotiate realistically with contractors, and made possible the design of appropriate structures for the varied climates.

~Dr. Stanley Quanbeck, former Medical Director of the Malagasy Lutheran Church's Medical Department

DESIGNS
for
HUMANITY

Kirk House Publishers
Burnsville, Minnesota

DESIGNS *for* HUMANITY

Reflections on Over 50 Years as a Master Builder
Dedicated to Meeting Basic Human Needs

Poul Bertelsen

First Printing: April 2025
First Edition

Paperback ISBN: 978-1-959681-79-3
eBook ISBN: 978-1-959681-81-6
Hardcover ISBN: 978-1-959681-80-9

LCCN: 2025903975

Interior and cover design by Ann Aubitz
Cover Image by Heather Beal
Author headshot by Thure Krarup

Published by Kirk House Publishers
1250 E 115th Street
Burnsville, MN 55337
kirkhousepublishers.com
612-781-2815

ACKNOWLEDGMENTS

I would like to thank the friends, colleagues and family members who have encouraged me to write this book as a follow up to *Design & Dignity*, which was published in 2012. Shortcomings in that book were likely that it attempted to cover too much and thus also became too long. It began as a memoir for me, but it evolved into a book aptly described by the subtitle "The Birth and Development of MSAADA Architects". For it also covered the history of the nonprofit architectural service organization that I cofounded in 1980.

This book focuses on what a lifetime of being involved as an architect in the developing world has taught me and it provides lessons that hopefully might be useful for other architects and building engineers who are working and serving in that so interesting part of the world. But maybe it might be of some interest also to others wanting to serve in the developing world.

My thanks for making this book a reality goes first to Heather Beal. For after she was contributing editor for *Design & Dignity*, she became part of creating the outline for this book. As a published author and journalist specializing in the design and construction of the built environment for over 30 years, Heather also contributed valuable input and advice later for the manuscript and editing.

After my successor as Executive Director of Msaada Architects, W. Jerry Murray, provided additional input, Karsten Potts made the edits. His education plus his working in and for Eastern Africa through non-profit humanitarian organizations was valuable for this role. My granddaughter, Ella Bradburn, assisted in preparing the pictures and drawings for publication.

My thanks next go to Kirk House Publishers for their support in publishing this book after they also published *Design & Dignity*.

Last but certainly not least, lots of thanks go to my wife Susanna and to our three children and their families who have brought so much joy and meaning to my life and who have been willing to accept the extensive traveling my involvement in mostly the developing world through Msaada Architects required over a period of four decades.

TABLE OF CONTENTS

FOREWORD

In my architectural career, I have been blessed by having several mentors: colleagues who took an avid interest in my professional development while sharing lessons from their personal experience. These mentors shaped me into not only being a better architect, but also into being a better person. Poul Bertelsen was my first.

After I graduated from the Master of Architecture program at the University of Minnesota, there was an economic recession, so jobs were hard to find. I wanted to stay in the Twin Cities, so I was fortunate to find consulting work with architectural firms doing drafting, model building and the like. Msaada was one of those firms.

The work for Msaada was different than anything for which I had been trained. We used metric scales and interesting terminology like "Tyrolean rendering" and "ant guards." We were drawing simple structures that had a leanness to them — a leanness that was beautiful in its practical application and stewardship of resources.

After working part time with Msaada for almost two years, Poul asked if I would be interested in opening the Msaada office in Tanzania, East Africa. Not recognizing the invitation as God's calling at the time, I probably replied with: "Sure, why not?" I wasn't doing anything marvelous in the U.S. I was simply working, earning a living, and paying my bills.

So, I went. And by going, it changed my life.

For the first time in my young career, I experienced the true power of architecture. I discovered that our work as architects was not to glorify the designer, but to serve the inhabitants. Though I had been trained to be creative and push the envelope of design, I was now challenged to do "more with less". And in doing more, lives were changed and humanity itself was encouraged to develop a dignified existence.

Over those slightly more than eight years in Africa, Poul mentored me on his ideals of architecture, which are expressed in this book. Msaada was doing something in the world that no one else was doing at that time. There were lots of local and international architects certainly willing to work in the major cities. But the real work in the "bush" where well-built and well-designed buildings were most needed? This challenge was left to Msaada!

How do you accomplish so much with limited resources, a lack of building materials and an absence of skilled labor? Through tenacity and a belief in what God has called you to do. Poul certainly had both, which made him a tough mentor. Poul had a clear vision of what an architect should be doing in the world and if you failed in meeting that vision, you were the first to know.

For a young architect, being corrected is never welcome, but in the long run, it is essential to personal and professional growth. In many ways, Poul gave me the education that I never received while a student at the university. He taught me not just how to work, but how to work toward something that you believe in.

Though I left Msaada after 10 years and went into private practice in the U.S., I carried with me a well-established base of principles from Poul that have guided my career. Since returning to Msaada and having the opportunity to meet other architects who, after me, were also mentored by Poul, I recognize one common thread: Msaada and Poul Bertelsen changed their lives.

As you read this book, may you be blessed and challenged. May your mind be opened, and your heart filled with a desire to use your chosen profession to not simply survive, but to serve.

~**W. Jerry Murray** Executive Director - Msaada Architects, 2020-2024.

CONTRIBUTOR'S PREFACE

As I was reviewing Poul's preliminary manuscript for this book, the photo I took of three boys at The Center for Street Children in Nairobi kept returning to my mind. To me, these boys represent the "humanity" behind the designs Msaada Architects has created over the past 40+ years.

I believe *Designs for Humanity* is distinct in the way it illustrates how deeply rooted Msaada Architects' work is in the "anthropology of place." Poul Bertelsen illustrates the complexity of human relationships associated with global design projects by describing how the local client in the developing world, the users, and the Western-world funders can have very different ideas about what a building should be and why it needs to be built.

The experiences and insights Poul shares in this book show how Msaada Architects' team addresses the priorities of *all the people* involved in a project and, most crucially, considers the needs of those who will work, live, visit, operate and maintain a facility long after an inauguration ceremony has occurred. Msaada Architects' team members ask:

- Who will own, occupy, visit, maintain, and provide funding for the construction and ongoing operation of this facility?
- Why is this facility important for the people whose lives it will touch?
- How can it meet unmet, essential human needs?
- What activities will transpire here?
- What materials, resources, and skills are available locally and which of these are appropriate to integrate into the design?

- How can this facility have a lasting, positive impact on its inhabitants and its community?

After I took the photo now featured on the cover of *Designs for Humanity*, a senior staff member at The Center for Street Children explained that these youth had been "glue boys." When she told me what lengths they — and other children at The Center — had needed to go to in order to survive on the streets of Nairobi, it broke my heart.

To me, the image of these boys, leaning toward each other and looking straight into the camera, conveys both a sense of what they had been through and what is in front of them.

Msaada Architects designed the buildings on this educational campus. As I toured each structure, listened to the stories of the staff, and met the children, it was clear that The Center offered them more than a formal education. It gave them hope, shelter, refuge, sustenance, camaraderie in a safe environment where they were valued, and opportunities for carefree play.

~Heather Beal, 2024

INTRODUCTION

I consider myself a very privileged individual, who has been fortunate to blend meaningfully my professional and my private life. A life which ended up being dedicated — after I had become what I prefer to call a **Social Justice Christian** — to serving as an architect in the developing world. In 2012, my earlier book, *Design & Dignity,* dealt with how Msaada Architects had served on church-sponsored building projects in the developing world for over 30 years, and with me having done so before that for a bit over a year in Nigeria and 6 years in Tanzania.

This book is, therefore, based on me now having served even longer in the developing world with what I have come to consider a lifelong vocation. Something I seemingly was called to do, even though that was not how I looked at it, when I initially went to Africa, after I reluctantly had agreed to become a **missionary architect.**

This calling later led me to co-founding Msaada Architects in 1980, together with two passive partners, who contributed as volunteer board members and provided financial expertise. Also note how this book relates to specifically Msaada Architects as primarily a recording of how it was founded and how it operated, served, and functioned for its initial four decades when I was the Executive Director.

I should add for clarification how somebody may suggest that I maybe shouldn't professionally mix my architectural opinions with what I believe as a person of Christian faith. But I can't separate the two because for me they are integrally related. Similarly, I cannot ignore how I am a definite product of having grown up in progressive Scandinavia in the middle of the last century.

Msaada, a Swahili word meaning "assistance," was used originally as an acronym for a rather long, complicated name in English. That long name was later dropped. But all-caps for Msaada continued to be used until the name was changed in late 2019 to be **Msaada Architects**. That coincided with when I retired as Executive Director and with W. Jerry Murray becoming my immediate successor. I am therefore now involved only as a part-time general consultant to the organization as might be required or desired.

As a nonprofit registered in Minnesota, Msaada has often by others been referred to as a Christian architecture and engineering firm. But today, where it often is difficult to define what something labeled "Christian" truly means, I prefer **calling it a ministry, which, with a focus on Christian values, provides Architectural and Engineering services for churches, missions, and related organizations in primarily the developing world.**

What Msaada Architects does, and what I was involved with earlier as a missionary architect, was based on what I heard stated many years ago, namely that **after being converted to Christ, we must be converted to the World** — to share and be involved also with our global neighbors. I believe this is a life journey, where we who hope to qualify as being Christians must attempt to live as much as possible as Christ did. I am saying so, even though that has been a constant challenge my whole life. But one which also has made me aware that while living in service can be complicated, it mostly results in true joy. And while it might not be as financially lucrative to serve in the developing world as in the U.S. or Europe, such a career not only offers numerous non-monetary bonuses but also an extremely exciting and meaningful life, professionally and privately.

It is also attractive that in most parts of the world, architects are still working as **Master Builders** in the planning, designing, and implementation of building projects. Thus, Africa ended up not only inspiring me to transform my understanding of Christianity but also made me realize what I should do as an architect and in that process affirm the important root of architecture as it has been practiced by generations of Master Builders.

This book is therefore my attempt to share what I have learned from a lifetime working and serving as a nonprofit architect in the developing world — although I will certainly not assume to have all the answers. But I hope my experiences might be of some value to others who want to use a background as an architect or a building engineer to serve both neighbors nearby as well as our global neighbors.

I further hope the book might also inspire architects and building engineers wanting to shift focus in the U.S. to work on **Public Interest and Humanitarian Design** projects, and that it might guide architects seeking to regain the parts of the project planning, design, and building process that they (at least as I see it) seem largely to have lost here in the U.S. This book therefore offers my literary mentorship to those reading it.

Also note that me working as an architect in Denmark for a few years before I went overseas gave me the confidence to always feel, that if I could not continue what became a vocation for me in the developing world, I should be able to return to work in the Western world. I have thus often told young architects and engineers wanting to join Msaada with primarily the intent to work overseas, how they should preferably work in their own country for a few years before going overseas.

My professional background is being a Registered Architect (RA) in Denmark, and thus I can practice in most EU countries. In the U.S. I am an American Institute of Architects (AIA) International Associate. However, I believe that my having spent over five decades working in the developing world — or serving that part of the world from the Western World as an architect — has given me experiences that might be valuable for others with an interest in serving in that so different but also so very interesting part of the world.

This book therefore shows and refers to different types of projects located in countries across the developing world, as well as a few projects in other parts of the world. For Msaada Architects has been fortunate to serve on a wide range of projects worldwide while emphasizing to serve projects for Christian churches, missions, and related organizations. Over the years, many people have believed this emphasis meant that Msaada only designs buildings with spaces for Christian worship.

However, about 75% of Msaada's project involvement has been with educational or medical facilities. Buildings for worship are the largest project group after that and include over 50 churches with a seating capacity from a few hundred to three thousand people. Other projects in the developing world include a variety of facilities, all built primarily to provide services that should assist in enhancing the lives of our global neighbors.

I would have preferred it if the project photos in this book were of a higher quality. But photographing completed projects was not always given the attention by Msaada, it should merit. So, I now recommend that time always be given to properly photographing completed projects to effectively illustrate our "stories" about those projects when building on cumulative knowledge as professionals, even when serving primarily on low-cost projects in the developing world, as Msaada has mostly done.

I believe that requires not only spending more time and effort in the future to ensure good quality pictures of projects done. For it also requires tolerance from the readers of this book for the at times rather low-quality copies of some of the pictures included for project samples referred to.

Further note how both photos and drawings in this book are not located next to the relevant texts of projects referred to, but instead they are at the end of each chapter listed in the order the projects have been referred to. Also, there aren't visuals for all projects referred to.

PART ONE

MASTER BUILDERS

CHAPTER 1

WHY MASTER BUILDERS?

Note importantly related to the content of this book, how, the projects done in the past by Msaada Architects in the developing world, as well as those I was involved with in Nigeria and Tanzania as a missionary architect, have all been based on serving in the century-old traditional role of architects being master builders.

For practical reasons note also, how I will only use the name Msaada Architects in this book, even when referring to matters before the name was officially changed from MSAADA Architects at the end of 2019. With the exception being that I will keep the original name, when that is referred to in quotes.

Architects as Master Builders

Thus, my clear conviction when Msaada Architects was founded that it should serve as a traditional Master Builder. I am using that specific term, even though I believe one never becomes a true master of anything. I am therefore using it with the understanding that there also is some satisfaction in never reaching perfection. I also believe that architects should never forget that our profession originates from persons who were the designing and coordinating head builders of projects — with the important emphasis on the functional and aesthetic parts of a new structure — and we should thus also keep in mind how architects traditionally simply were known and served as Master Builders.

I have, therefore, been using this understanding in Msaada Architects partly because I personally believe in architects still being master builders. I was further expected to use that understanding in my work as a missionary architect in Nigeria and Tanzania. But I have also continued to use the term Master Builder in Msaada because that was indeed how architects mostly worked in my home country, Denmark, when I began my professional career there in the mid-1960s.

At that time, architects were usually the clients' central professional consultants on building projects. Our work included hiring other required consultants, such as various engineers, and afterward arranging and supervising the tendering/bidding process for construction work in addition to doing actual construction observation and supervision. All of this was naturally done based on appropriate approval by the clients, while always keeping their best interests in mind. When mentioning that, I must hurry to add that there have also been some changes regarding how architects work in Denmark today, as there have been changes for colleagues here in the U.S.

Based on what I have experienced personally, the changes seem to be more extensive though here in the U.S. From what I understand; it has become more the norm here that building projects are managed and controlled by developers or general building contractors and not by architects. This is something which I have not experienced personally, as being the case anywhere else in the close to 50 countries where I have had the pleasure — or blessing as I prefer to call it — of serving as an architect.

Furthermore, in addition to that background information regarding my use of the term Master Builder, it might be helpful to also mention how my education to become an architect in Denmark was not through the more academic route. Instead, it was based on the "nuts and bolts" approach to architecture and building construction. Further, I was required to have worked for some time in one of the construction trades as an apprentice, and I also had to have passed the qualifying test in that trade before getting my diploma. This requirement was also based on how architecture traditionally in Denmark was a so-called liberal profession before that was changed later by EU rules.

My architectural and building construction education was developed further by me commencing my professional career with working for 3 years as kind of an architectural apprentice in what was, at that time, a larger, important architectural firm in Denmark.

Further, in Msaada Architects, we have usually been involved with matters at the beginning of projects in the developing world, which colleagues in the Western world does not usually deal with. Because, if agreed upon by the client, Msaada Architects has always preferred to provide services from the beginning of design through the full completion of construction. For this places the architect in the important central coordinating role of advising and serving the client from the time an idea for a building project is envisioned until construction is fully completed and the doors are opened.

Therefore, by describing how Msaada Architects became uniquely qualified for the work it does, I hope this book will become a guide for other architects (or architectural students) who want to complete building projects that meet basic human needs in the developing world. Or, as stated in the Introduction, it might even inspire architects working in the U.S. to reclaim some of what I believe the profession seems to have lost in this country.

Having an expanded role as Master Builder has meant, though, that Msaada Architects often has needed to take risks and to be ready to do so beyond what many architects in the U.S. today seem to be ready for. This has not only been to uphold the role of the Master Builder but also to provide the kind of assistance that is often required to make projects materialize in the developing world, and to do so in ways that will ensure those projects provide appropriate physical spaces for important life-enhancing services for our global neighbors.

Related to that, I once saw the following suggestions for running a truly worthwhile organization. I have put those suggestions into practice throughout my career and view them as words to live by to this day:

Risk more than others think is safe,
Care more than others think is wise,
Dream more than others think is practical.... and
Expect more than others think is possible!

Looking back on Msaada Architects' history, it is clear to me, how often I not only needed to take **risks** that could be scary to face but also needed to **care, dream,** and **expect** more than I felt was easy or feasible. There were also times when I had to do something that I was not only uncomfortable with, but which also made me personally more vulnerable, all to keep Msaada functioning as a true service organization for four decades. But life has also taught me that **opportunities usually come with challenges**. For me, acting on these opportunities and tackling related challenges are what it means **for life to truly be experienced and not just lived**.

I have personally learned that following this philosophy can result in an extremely meaningful experience for Western architects or building engineers working in the developing world. I recognize that while others might not be motivated by what I understand as Christian values, these, too, have positively and very meaningfully added to my life's journey. I also believe that **"we do not choose our lives. Instead, they choose us,"** as I once saw described by a Native American saying.

It might not be possible to always compare what Msaada Architects does in other parts of the world with how building projects are handled in the U.S. However, the experience my co-workers at Msaada and I have had in completing a few U.S. projects showed us that working as a Master Builder here could be much like the role, we have had on projects overseas. We also learned this meant Msaada often had to take responsibility, though, and accept possible liabilities that U.S. architects usually might not have to face.

Building contractors were comfortable with this arrangement, and so were the clients, especially when we ensured such projects were built cost-effectively without sacrificing the quality of the final product. Additionally, it is worth noting that although Msaada to date has been blessed to see close to one thousand projects implemented, we have never been involved in a court case or even in arbitration with clients or building contractors.

Further about my Personal Background
I ended up as a missionary architect in Nigeria and Tanzania after having had a rather promising start as a young architect in Denmark in the mid-to-late 1960s. After I initially had worked as mentioned earlier for three years as an apprentice in an architectural firm with about 60 employees, which was then a reasonably sized firm in my home country, I was offered the chance to take charge of a small branch office of that firm in a neighboring town.

That was after I had otherwise started making plans for supplementing my professional education, which was called a diploma then but a bachelor's degree now, after Denmark had to coordinate its educational system with those of other EU countries. Such graduate studies would lead to the equivalent of a Master of Architecture degree in the U.S. However, accepting the leadership of the branch office meant I had to drop my plans — at that time — for further formal studies.

Managing the branch office lasted for only about a year, though, as I developed a strong desire to try something different geographically. That was also based on a growing feeling that I maybe was too young to already have a rather settled professional role, albeit in a reputable architectural firm, while still having not yet fully reached my late twenties. That desire to do something different was supported by the already mentioned fact that my formal education, which centered on the "nuts and bolts" approach to architecture, had benefitted from that during my three years as an architectural apprentice, I also had worked frequently as a draftsman on national design competition projects for the studio's chief architect, who won several prestigious Danish architectural design competitions.

Thus, I decided to apply for a job in two other countries, including one in London, which I specifically hoped to get because I wanted to also emphasize learning better English. I had, as a student, studied more German than English as a second language. Later, I was able to practice reading and speaking English when I agreed, rather reluctantly, to a proposal for me to go to Nigeria together with three very close friends. In preparation for that, we spent a semester at Selly Oak Church Colleges in Birmingham, U.K., studying missiology, Islam, Africa, and related international graduate coursework.

Shortly after I had agreed to become a missionary architect in Nigeria, I received an offer for the job I had applied for in London. My life was totally turned upside down by the decision to instead serve in Nigeria, as this led to me doing projects in the developing world that I felt were more needed than those I had worked on in Denmark and what I likely would have done in London. And while going to Nigeria meant significantly reduced financial earnings, this experience further strengthened and transformed my Christian faith.

After a bit more than a year in Nigeria, I married my American wife Susanna in mid-1971, and I then worked for a short time in Ohio. But I also spent a semester completing courses at Ohio State University with the goal to then earn a graduate degree in architecture, as I had earlier hoped to do in Denmark. However, such plans were interrupted (again) when I learned that the Danish Mission Society (DMS) was looking for an architect to develop an Architectural/Engineering department in the national central office of the Evangelical Lutheran Church in Tanzania (ELCT).

That seemed like a great opportunity to work for a much larger national Lutheran Church in Africa than the one I'd served in Nigeria. Based on the time I had worked already in Denmark, Nigeria, and the U.S., I was already getting quite familiar with much of what was taught in graduate school. All these factors thus contributed to Susanna's and my decision to take off for Tanzania at the very outset of 1973.

I have never regretted that decision, for the six years in Tanzania ended up being some of the best years of my life, partly because that experience was the basis for founding Msaada Architects in 1980. This is something that became a true personal blessing, though often also a very challenging one, to be in charge of this nonprofit firm for about 40 years as executive director and principal architect until the end of 2019.

So, I never ended up fully earning a graduate degree, even though, for close to a decade, I was one of two practicing architects called "Professor in Practice," who taught a yearly spring half-semester graduate course at the University of Minnesota's School of Architecture in the College of Design. This course used projects completed by us — the two instructors — as examples for study and analysis by the students. They were, therefore, asked to prepare and present how they would approach the usually rather complicated design requests that we had been given by our clients.

A week later, the students shared their suggestions for how they might address the design challenges given, followed by us, the instructors, revealing to the students our actual design solutions. I taught one day a week while somebody else taught another day that same week. To give variety (or contrast) for the students, the other practicing architect was either doing projects in the U.S. or was involved with "fancier," more expensive, and elaborate projects abroad, while I presented projects done by Msaada Architects in the developing world. Msaada's projects were, comparatively, accomplished for a fraction of the monetary cost.

The fact that my teaching started two years before *Design & Dignity* was published in late 2012 prompted the inclusion of two chapters titled "*Dignified Development and Growth in the Developing World*" as well as "*How Msaada Works and Serves*," which addressed how the organization had — by then — been able to get about 750 projects built and to have done so despite the low fees received. The low fees are due mainly to the usually much lower construction costs in the developing world than in the Western world, while the number of completed projects by Msaada now is close to 1,000.

My experience teaching at the University of Minnesota also inspired the idea that my earlier book should maybe be followed by a book like this. For I much appreciated the opportunity to share with U.S. architectural graduate students how they don't need to follow what most other architects do to have a solid and meaningful professional career.

The experience at the University of Minnesota also affirmed my personal belief that it may be more important to seek and employ useful skills already obtained than to continue seeking more diplomas or degrees. That belief of mine is influenced by my having been extremely blessed to have had many valuable mentors who have taught me a lot in what I often tend to think of as the "university of life."

Such mentors include the Chief of Studio Architect, whom I worked under during my three-year architectural apprenticeship in Denmark: Poul Erik Thyrring. When facing challenging design situations throughout my career, I have often thought: "How would Thyrring address this?"

The General Secretary of the Evangelical Lutheran Church in Tanzania (ELCT), Joel Ngeiyamu, was the driving force behind the desire to turn an already existing Building Department into a full Architectural/Engineering Department in the headquarters of that large national church. This was to ensure that the many building projects done by that church body would be appropriately designed and completed with quality construction as economically as possible. I therefore worked very closely with Joel in Tanzania and, thus, also learned so much culturally from him. So later, when facing cultural challenges, I often thought: "How might Ngeiyamu suggest I should handle this situation?"

Understanding the Developing World

In addition to Msaada Architects providing professional architectural and engineering (A/E) services for mostly church-sponsored building projects in the developing world, we have also made efforts to assist in creating a better understanding of that world in the West. Related to Africa, for example, many in the Western world envision the continent as being different from how I have experienced it. Although, for example, TV series often concentrate on the rich wildlife, it is the people who make it so unique. People who have earlier had highly developed ancient civilizations in several places on their continent.

I have also observed how many in the Western world believe Africa to be a homogeneous continent. They are unaware that it has many differences among its unique countries, as I personally have experienced by living in both Nigeria and Tanzania. Later, I further observed these differences when Msaada served in many additional African countries, which each have their own cultures that are usually a mixture of the traditional (mostly rural areas) and the modern world (mostly bigger cities).

While India is still considered a developing country, there are many who have predicted recently that India might soon be a major nation for the rest of the world to deal with economically and otherwise. And that although India, as I see it, even more than the countries of Africa, has a by far too great inequality between those citizens living in the big cities and those who live in the rural areas of that large country. So, there is still a need for much development in India.

Important as a Master Builder in the Developing World

There are many examples where Msaada Architects' ability to provide a design with cost estimates reliably and quickly made it possible for a project in the developing world to be funded by a donor. There have also been many times when Msaada Architects' ability to provide expertise and management during a project's construction phase made it possible for construction to be done well and cost-effectively. In fact, we have had over 95% of Msaada's A/E projects completed within budgets, and we are thankful for this. But completing projects on time in the developing world is much more complicated!

Architects (or building engineers) who are excited about and feel committed to serving as Master Builders in other parts of the world will probably also find it important to travel to and learn within that part of the world, even when doing so might be uncomfortable. For that is what I have experienced in new cultures before starting to work there. As mentioned earlier, I have also learned that taking risks and being personally vulnerable is a definite part of serving in the developing world. So, maybe this approach also can be used for projects in the U.S. to expand the architects' role in building projects here.

Why are there not more Master Builders in the U.S.?
The legal climate with excessive litigation has likely contributed to what I see as the comparatively shrinking role of architects in the U.S. Or at least a much more limited role than what I experienced as a young architect-to-be in Denmark and more limited than what I later have experienced in many other countries in the world.

Historically, architects have been involved with all aspects of the process, from when a project is visualized through its planning, design, and implementation. And shouldn't an architect ideally know more than how to design functional and attractive buildings, as seems often today to be the extent of architectural services on projects here in the U.S.?

There might, of course, be architects with such great artistic and creative skills that they can focus on doing concept designs, both for their own benefit and for that of their society. But for the kind of projects Msaada Architects has completed, and for those I served on before that organization was founded, I believe architectural services should, among other things, also include serious consideration of and even some responsibility for ensuring that the client's budgeted project costs are being kept.

In the developing world, that cost depends extensively on the kind of materials used and the use of well-known building technologies or new ones. Shouldn't this also be the case here in the U.S.? I have often told colleagues that if they apply what Msaada Architects is doing to what architects here can do also, they might avoid getting stuck in "siloes of specialization." For I have personally always felt being a Master Builder has been not only challenging in the developing world most of the time but also very enjoyable and extremely meaningful.

CHAPTER 2

HUMANITARIAN AND PUBLIC INTEREST DESIGNS

The awakening of what is now referred to as "**Humanitarian Design** and/or **"Public Interest Design"** in the U.S. is based on what I have always understood as being essential. Namely, building designs should focus on **intelligently maximizing a project's ability to meet fundamental human needs.** So Msaada Architects — and I personally, before that organization was founded — completed public interest and humanitarian designs prior to the use of these terms, making Msaada likely an early leader in these movements before these phrases became commonly known and used.

For further clarification, though, I will refer to the present Wikipedia interpretation of Public Interest Design, which will likely continue to be changed and updated:

*"**Public interest design** is a human-centered[1] and participatory design practice[2] that places emphasis on the "triple bottom line" of sustainable design that includes ecological, economic, and social issues and on designing products, structures, and systems that address issues such as economic development and the preservation of the environment. Projects incorporating public interest design focus on the general good of the local citizens with a fundamentally collaborative perspective.[3]"*

Also, Humanitarian Design is presently defined as follows by Wikipedia:

*"**Humanitarian design** is a term that can be used to describe the process of designing products, services, or systems for populations affected by natural and/or human-made disasters."*

I must add, though, how I personally use that term to describe designs by architects and building engineers that more broadly serve matters of real importance for the lives of both our local as well as our global neighbors.

What Msaada Architects has traditionally Emphasized

It is interesting how terminology develops over time, for I have often been asked if Msaada Architects' designs are "**green**." My answer has usually been, "Yes, even before this term was coined and became so common in the Western world." Projects in the developing world must optimize the value of money spent. Accomplishing this goal often overlaps with green design principles, such as efficiently using locally sourced materials and employing techniques and technologies for conserving energy and water.

Msaada Architects was founded to serve primarily on "**church-sponsored projects**" in the developing world. We have traditionally defined "church-sponsored projects" as ones that are initiated by and implemented by indigenous churches with (most often) financial assistance from missions or other church-related organizations based in the Western world. As founder and the initial Executive Director of Msaada, I am respectfully convinced that such projects in the developing world are completed more efficiently and with more value for the project money spent than is usually the case for projects funded and implemented by, for example, governments.

My earlier book, *Design & Dignity*, addresses this topic in greater detail. It also includes stories regarding how such projects were planned, designed, and implemented.

However, as stated in the Introduction, this present book's objective is to provide — illustrated by many project examples — more specific suggestions for how architects or engineers from the Western world can work and serve on projects in the developing world. It is based on what is now more than five decades of my personal experiences, beginning with me being in Nigeria for a bit more than a year in 1970-71.

But it is supplemented with information received from clients related to services provided. I should regarding that likely add, how there are duplications of such information from Design & Dignity but usually in a shorter reduced form in this book.

Preparing for Projects in the Developing World

There is a rather steep learning curve for architects (or engineers) who previously have not worked in the developing world. Since projects should appropriately relate to the local culture and customs, architects must initially learn about these and about local materials and building techniques, for it is usually more economical to use well-known, indigenous building techniques and materials. This also makes practical sense because members of the local labor force usually operate, repair, and maintain the new buildings.

Personally, I don't know how I could have founded Msaada Architects and been responsible for the completion of so many projects throughout the developing world without my earlier experiences in Nigeria and Tanzania. Other staff members have also experienced the value of working overseas so that they can immerse themselves in the culture and traditions of the places where projects are located.

As an example, my valued colleague for many years, Scott Williams, worked in Msaada's Madagascar and Kenya area offices for three years before he became Chief of Studio Architect in Msaada's Minnesota home office. He then went on to work for about three decades in that role, which included project visits to countries in the developing world.

The initial idea for creating Msaada Architects came mostly from fellow missionaries and indigenous colleagues of mine in Tanzania. They suggested that perhaps I should consider doing something like that after my service in the national Lutheran Church's central office in Tanzania was completed. They pointed out how such an organization could then serve Christian churches more broadly (denominationally and geographically) than the A/E Department of the Evangelical Lutheran Church in Tanzania.

So, in short, the best preparation for architects (or engineers) from the Western world who want to serve in the developing world is, I believe, to spend some quality time living in the countries where they want to work. This reduces the time typically required for doing cultural and other research prior to the start of planning and design. There are, unfortunately, too many examples of projects being done in the developing world that were too heavily based on design criteria in the Western world. These projects, in the worst cases, might become "White Elephants," and there is no need for more of these!

It is thus important for Western architects and engineers serving on projects in the developing world to realize how planning and design must be done with sensitivity and the best possible cultural understanding. Only then can the projects be expected to have the significant positive impact they should have on the people for whom they are being built. After working for so long in and with the developing world, I can further testify to how it is only with a good knowledge of all the environmental and cultural factors influencing the design of a project that architects and engineers are truly able to feel the personal satisfaction that comes from doing something worthwhile and meaningful.

However, while you can learn to appreciate and understand a great deal about another culture, don't make the mistake of believing that you are as knowledgeable as the local indigenous population. Although there is (and should be) space for new and different designs as well as innovative building techniques and materials in the developing world, there have been too many examples where designs by Western architects and engineers have been built and later found to be too com-plicated for the new building owners to use and maintain. That is also because the expertise in dealing with new building techniques and cer-tain materials may no longer be easily available after completed facili-ties are handed over to their future users.

A critical factor when designing buildings in the developing world includes significantly ensuring they are designed to be structurally sound so they will have long life spans. Further, always consider how the need for future maintenance can be minimized, for while no build-ings can be designed to be completely maintenance free, the repair and maintenance of buildings in the developing world continues to be a great challenge.

It was not so terribly long ago that colonial rule ended in most parts of the developing world. So, the people using new buildings had by then become accustomed to having structures designed and built with fund-ing from outside donors, often without sufficient consideration for how the buildings would be used, operated, and maintained. Thus, whether a new building was a medical, educational, or worship facility, the users learned to fit themselves into the available spaces. This was far from an ideal situation, as the users had to live with any functional deficiencies of a building long after its doors were opened.

Two Big Ears and One Small Mouth
The situation I just described has improved much in recent years. Still, architects must ensure that the design process in the developing world begins with a conversation instead of too quickly "giving" clients pro-posed design suggestions. For this conversation to be productive, I have found that the architect should have **two big ears and one small mouth,** for as the saying goes, "**knowledge speaks while wisdom listens**."

When architects begin by listening well, they can then also ask bet-ter questions and draw out a more detailed understanding of what the client truly wants or needs. This information, then, is to be evaluated in relation to what is financially and logistically possible. Only after completing these tasks should the architect start making actual concept design proposals.

An experience I had related to a new **Lutheran Church Centre in the suburb of Jerusalem in Nairobi,** Kenya, reinforced for me the value of listening. That centre had a worship space as well as rooms for local community functions, plus the head office of the ELCT Kenya Synod. The project was developed when I oversaw the A/E Department at the central office of the Evangelical Lutheran Church in Tanzania (ELCT). During the opening ceremony of the new centre, I recall appreciating that Tanzania's Lutheran Church's General Secretary stressed how when the conversation about the project's design program commenced, I did not begin by talking. Instead, I started out asking many questions about how the new buildings were expected to function and be used.

What Clients Really Might Require

I have also learned how architects working in the developing world should not always provide clients with **exactly what they ask for** but instead should use the time during the design phase to help them better understand what good design entails, for there are times when **something different or even something less** can better suit the users' needs. This approach can also help bridge the gap that often exists between what the desires of the future users are for the projects in the developing world and their affordability. So, the design discussion should also address how to obtain the best value for the money to be invested in a building project.

If there ends up being a significant disagreement between what client representatives want and what the architect suggests for a design, however, then the architect's skills should be used by doing design work based on what the clients want when so feasible. After all, the clients are the ones who live with the impact of design decisions long after the building is first occupied, not the architect.

There are also times when architects serving in cultures, which they are not familiar with, might truly believe they understand what is needed or required for a project, only to realize later how wrong they were. Ideally, this realization should occur early in the planning and design process.

Additional Considerations
On most Msaada projects, there have usually been two sets of client representatives: one being a local client partner serving as the project holder and future "user" of a new facility and the other being an outside client partner serving as a "donor" who will cover part or all the project cost. As a result, there are often conflicts between what the project holder expects to be accomplished, and the limits set by the project budget.

Thus, before creating concept designs, an efficient way to get somewhere quickly is to start working with **space schedules and related rough cost estimates**. This work should usually begin immediately after a design program has been tentatively outlined. Such an approach helps guarantee the best and most financially feasible result because the schedules and related cost estimates enable the future users and a donor to intelligently discuss what is possible to do financially.

Over the years, a significant challenge for Msaada Architects has been one that is also common in other parts of the world, namely how A/E projects being served at any time seem to follow a mountain/valley-like pattern. Thus, I often have been concerned about considering a new project request when we were perhaps almost too busy already.

While an essential part of Msaada Architects' original creation was based on our desire to respond to specific needs, it can be difficult to decide when to stop responding further to those needs while working in the developing world. Thus, at Msaada, we have realized that for a non-profit organization to continue to meet client needs effectively and affordably, it should not become too big, as this usually leads to substantially increased overhead costs. So, it can at times be difficult to decide when it is possible to properly handle another project.

To truly serve local churches in the developing world, architects should also assist them in setting realistic project goals based on the extent that potential clients are ready to accept this advice. Additionally, it has been encouraging to experience how many churches in the developing world coordinate their planning of development projects with those of local governments, something that is usually mutually beneficial.

These considerations related to Msaada Architects' services have allowed us to truly provide **"Msaada,"** meaning "assistance" in Swahili. These considerations parallel what local churches and their congregations in the developing world usually do themselves by assisting beyond their own members. In fact, it seems that **"instead of having a social ethic, they tend to BE a social ethic,"** as I once saw it expressed so very well.

This relates to something that I most appreciate about the developing world, namely the sense of community that you find almost everywhere. I find this is especially true in Africa. For it is usually natural for African Christians and their church congregations to always share what they have with others, even outside of their own community. They are most willing to do so to an extent beyond what we seem to be ready for in the Western world. In this way, the **"community doesn't just create abundance, but it instead becomes a source of abundance,"** as I have heard somebody suggest, and which is not as dependent on material abundance and wealth, as we in the Western world too often seem to believe or feel is required.

After these considerations, it seems relevant to also refer to how it is becoming so important here in the U.S. to emphasize **diversity, equality, and inclusion (DEI).** But doing so seems to have been a practiced norm for a long time in the developing world.

Working Backwards

"It is perfectly true, as philosophers say, that life must be understood backwards. But they forget the other proposition, that it must be lived forwards." — *Søren Kierkegaard.*

I have always appreciated this quote by the 19th-century Danish Christian philosopher and pastor. As life is to be lived forwards, we architects must do our best to understand how this also applies to the users of facilities we design and get built.

I learned the importance of this when working in another culture — initially, during my short time in Nigeria and, later, during the six years I was living and working in Tanzania. The significance of these words deepened as I broadened my knowledge and experience after Msaada Architects was founded. I've seen how asking clients what they need to accomplish by constructing a building and asking how much money and time they have available usually "opens the door" to work backwards, so to speak, in the design process.

Therefore, doing this can be a preferable way to clarify how a certain amount of money available for capital investment in a project can best be used to accomplish what the clients want or need, for the available funds can then simply be used to determine what the maximum size a total floor area can be for a proposed new building.

Lutheran Church Centre in the suburb of Jerusalem in Nairobi, Kenya

CHAPTER 3

WHAT IT MIGHT TAKE TO ENSURE PROJECTS MATERIALIZE

Too many envisioned projects in the developing world never materialize. Reasons for that vary, but the most common one seems to be an inability to start planning based on what realistically can be accomplished. Msaada Architects has experienced numerous situations where a local client in the developing world wanted to do a project for which it seemed difficult or even impossible to secure funding. We have then usually learned not to get involved in these cases and to explain to a potential client our reason for that.

We have also been part of projects initiated by somebody from the Western world who wanted to do something in the developing world without having properly checked into what is needed or desired locally — or maybe even without being realistic about what they, as a Western organization, could assist with and support financially.

Start with Something Realistic
Ensuring that projects in the developing world meet the requirements and expectations of both sets of clients is a constant challenge. I have often sat with persons involved in a project in, for example, Africa or

India and explained what I believed would be acceptable for a new project to be funded by donors in the Western world. And I have sat in the opposite part of the world and advocated for what truly might be needed or required by our global neighbors in the developing world.

A complicated example was a new **Teacher's Training College at Mwenge** in Tanzania, which started out with unrealistic expectations by a Roman Catholic Missionary Sister from the U.K., who was the driving force behind it. When she provided the design program information, we stressed how she wanted a higher standard than what an institution like that normally has in Africa. She then informed us how the Minister of Development in the U.K. government supposedly supported the project, so we should not worry about anything. However, when she realized later how expensive the project would be, and she did not have the U.K. Minister's support anyway, she asked Msaada's Tanzania office how they could believe she would be able to pay for something like that, "for funds from bake sales in the U.K.?"

The project had fortunately also been sent for possible funding assistance to Misereor, a Roman Catholic German organization supporting projects in the developing world, which Msaada had already worked with extensively. Thus, I was asked to come and discuss the project at their office in Germany. It was embarrassing to be told how they thought I should know what the funding limitations were for a project like this. I thus had to gently tell them what the U.K. Sister had said, and it was then suggested that as the project was truly needed, Msaada should redesign it based on the usual standards for Teacher Training Colleges in Tanzania. The changed design was then fortunately accepted for funding by Misereor, and it was seen through to construction completion.

Another example of a conflict was related to Msaada Architects' restoration of an approximately 300-year-old **Church of Zion in Tranquebar,** India, when the question arose around which type of mortar would be used for masonry work. We settled on something that eventually was acceptable to all stakeholders and Msaada was affirmed in the advantage of initially seeing the ideas behind a project from the viewpoint of a building's future users and then adjusting those with the ideas of a Western donor.

For the funding agency in Denmark had involved an architectural expert in the restoration and renovation of old buildings in Denmark in the project. However, it became clear how that expertise could not just be transferred and applied to the project in India, even though this situation involved something that seemed otherwise not so notable as which mortar to use for masonry work. So, I had to take a definite stand against a well-known expert on the renovation of old Danish masonry buildings when he strongly suggested that only lime mortar should be used for restoration of masonry work, considering that is all that was available when the church was built originally.

In contrast, the Indians wanted to use cement mortar, which is usually most appropriate for the often-extreme weather conditions in Southern India. I thus suggested that we, as a compromise, might settle on using what is usually called "bastard mortar," a mixture of lime and cement mortar. I referred also to how such mortar is often used, especially on the west coast of Denmark, not for the restoration of centuries-old buildings, but for newer buildings because of the periodically severe weather conditions there.

After the restoration work was successfully completed, the Danish project donor organization published an article that included the following comments: **"The restoration of the Church of Zion has demonstrated that such work can be done and is manageable within a reasonable budget with the use of local labor and skills. The team who worked on the Church of Zion are prepared to work on similar renovation projects in Tranquebar."**

That quote was in reference to how Tranquebar as a former Danish trading post in South India needed more restoration work. Thus, the Danish professional architects' organization had suggested that such restoration work would require involvement by not only Danish architects, but likely also some Danish craftsmen. I therefore was put on the "blacklist" of that organization because the work Msaada did on the

Church of Zion project proved it was possible to do such restoration work with only limited involvement by a Danish architect and by no involvement of any Danish craftsmen.

When I had earlier been asked about my personal involvement in the project, I stated — as was the case — how that had amounted to maybe less than 10% of the total efforts. The remaining A/E services were provided mostly by Msaada's associate office in India, and the construction work was done by an Indian building contractor whom Msaada had collaborated with on other projects. Due to this prior relationship, we knew this contractor would do high-quality work.

However, that situation was contrary to what the professional architects' organization suggested for other restoration and renovation projects in Tranquebar. I was thus labeled a "blackleg." I learned of this when I arrived in Denmark and was told by an architectural journalist that he could not interview me anyway, as he had planned to do during my visit to my home country, due to me having been put on the mentioned "blacklist". Something which naturally surprised me greatly.

Let me therefore also add now how there are numerous projects where Msaada's willingness to accept the challenge of applying a creative and, at times, unorthodox approach to what was to be done resulted in projects being completed and done well. Such projects usually started out wrongly and thus needed to become more appropriate.

As an example, the **University Church in Maiduguri,** Nigeria, was to be used jointly by Roman Catholics, Anglicans, and Lutherans. Construction had already commenced when Msaada was asked to redesign the church using an already built a foundation for what was originally planned as a simple flat-roofed design done by another consultant. The finished building became an aesthetically pleasing church, where we used the existing foundation layout to create a design with interesting sloping roofs. The completed church was so well received that we did not even need to explain later why it looked as it did.

Design for What is Required

A new **Lutheran church in the 67 Ha Section of Antananarivo,** Madagascar, was redesigned by Msaada after a Norwegian architect had done the work pro bono. But neither the design nor the proposed building materials properly addressed that country's climatic conditions. Thus, the project ended up with additional costs exceeding what had been saved from the pro bono design services. As an interesting side comment, we learned recently how that church is now the home of a large major congregation of the national Malagasy Lutheran Church (FLM), with the result being, among other things, that its worship services often are broadcast by public radio and TV in Madagascar.

A new **Multi-Purpose Training Centre in Udaipur, Rajasthan,** India, provides an example of when the client, Church's Auxiliary for Social Action (CASA), wanted typical Rajasthani architectural façade detailing in the design, something they realized rather late. After construction had commenced based on a design by a local architect, Msaada was asked to change the design of the facades so the building would better reflect Rajasthani architecture.

A new **Lutheran church building in Faulkton, South Dakota,** was Msaada's first project for a congregation in the U.S. This project arose when the Northern European donor organizations which supported church-sponsored projects in the developing world all changed — almost overnight — from doing mostly bricks-and-mortar projects to focusing on funding programs instead. At that time, the large majority of Msaada's work was on projects funded by those organizations.

Msaada had at that time staff in the home office in Minnesota as well as in three area offices in Africa, plus an associate office in India. So, we needed to do something new. Thus, we offered to do projects periodically for places of worship in the U.S. The one in Faulkton was the first such project. The parish council presented us with three possible options: option one was to move the existing building to another location; option two was to build a new church; and option three was to convert an existing former hardware store into a space of worship.

During the conversation about which of those possibilities to use, a member of the building committee spoke strongly against renovating the former hardware store, explaining that if that solution was chosen, he would always recall what the original function of this space was while worshipping. That was after I had stressed how church architecture should add positively to the worship liturgy and that religious art should, if possible, be included as well. Gazing at such art can, at times, be a substitute for listening to sermons that might not always be that captivating.

After the design for building a new church was completed, we received this message from the congregation: **"A very special thank you for the work you have done so far for Our Savior Lutheran Church in designing our new church. You gave us directions and helped us believe that our dream of a new church could become a reality. We love the design and are now moving forward with our fundraising project. With God, all things are possible – Matthew 19:26."**

It was extra encouraging later to have construction of that new church completed in high quality and for a reasonable cost.

When the Architect's Idea of Need is Wrong

As mentioned earlier, I strongly recommend never giving the idea you understand another culture better than the indigenous people. My work in the developing world has underscored the reality of that numerous times. I will share just a few examples.

One instance occurred when Msaada was asked to work on a design for a proposed new **Lutheran Church in Kyiv, Ukraine.** I arrived in Kyiv with a preconceived idea of what the client needed. That changed the very first day I was in town, after the local Lutheran bishop and I had visited several churches of different denominations in that city. Instead of a modern design, it was made clear to me that a new Lutheran church needed to feature elements from existing Orthodox and Ukrainian Catholic Church buildings to be culturally relevant in Kyiv.

Unfortunately, project funding from the U.S. later became a problem, so I do not know if the project ever materialized, and it was already planned from the outset that Msaada's proposed concept design was to be passed on to a local architectural firm for further work and the hoped-for implementation of the project.

Msaada's assignment to design the rebuilding of the **St. Francois de Sales University Hospital in Port-au-Prince, Haiti,** provides another example where I felt I had a clear idea of what was needed only to again be proven wrong. This project arose after the existing hospital had been 80% to 90% destroyed during the January 2010 earthquake in Haiti. I suggested the hospital be rebuilt with multi-story buildings. This made sense, as the space at the site was limited. But the Haitians were not ready for that just after the earthquake and thus wanted only to build one-story buildings before we ended up settling on a compromise of double-story buildings!

A final example where I thought I had things figured out was when a large new **Roman Catholic Church in a suburb of Nairobi, Kenya,** was to be built. I suggested such a large church with rather expensive finishes seemed almost out of place in the neighborhood where it was to be located. But I was "put in my place" when an old parishioner stressed that while he and his fellow parishioners were of modest means and lived in simple homes, they wanted a beautiful space where they could worship their God. He then asked me whether that was any different from when large cathedrals were built in Europe hundreds of years ago and the general population were also mostly of modest means.

Management of Project Budgets

Msaada has done literally hundreds of projects in the developing world that were only completed after we ensured construction costs were kept within planned budgets. A very modest example was a new **"Jebavidu" at Siloom Girl's Boarding School** in India. This is a small chapel used not only by the Christian students and staff, but also by Hindus and Muslims. As is the case for many other Msaada projects, this structure was built within a fixed amount of available funds and designed to be as spacious as possible for its use based on that funding limitation.

The **Arcot Lutheran Church School Project (ALCSP)** in India is a large-scale example of how critical, accurate cost estimating and cost management are. As will be mentioned later, 90+ schools were done in 10 phases or clusters, with funding for each additional group of projects contingent upon the previous phase or cluster having been completed within budget.

A small **Lutheran Seminary Project in Almaty, Kazakhstan,** is one where a new national Lutheran Church already had a one-story office building for their administrative department and other functions. When a fixed amount of money was available to build a small seminary with classrooms, offices, and a chapel, those facilities were economically added on top of the already existing one-story building, which fortunately had been designed to support a second story.

After my visit to Almaty for that project, I learned the following from the U.S. missionary pastor behind the project: **"I think your suggested plans are absolutely wonderful. Thanks for your work and your God-given gifts applied to our needs in Almaty! As far as I am concerned, if you could see me now, you would see a wide smile. I pray that we will realize all of this. The sooner, the better!"**

After the project was rather quickly implemented, we received the following message from the area director of the U.S. mission supporting this church: **"The building looks great. It is coming together very well. I can't thank you enough for your work here. I am also glad you have been able to hold the line on the budget. It not only gives you credibility, but also our field staff when we ask for more money to build."**

Getting that project done well and quickly was partly because the congregation had an unemployed female Russian architect. We, therefore, arranged for her to be Clerk of Works (architect and/or building engineer doing construction observation/supervision), and we supervised her in doing that job via e-mail communication from our

Minnesota office. The project thus got built, and, as a fringe benefit, Msaada assisted in the capacity building of the Russian architect.

A problem often faced with a fixed project budget that must not be exceeded is agreeing to payment requests from the building contractor late in the construction process that exceed the value of the work done. For, while Msaada mostly proposes giving a payment advance to building contractors at the outset of construction work — to obtain the best possible tender/bid — advance payments should absolutely end when half of the construction is completed and when retention deductions start being made for all payments. Not following this simple rule just "opens the door wide" for serious problems.

Teacher's Training College at Mwenge, Tanzania

Church of Zion in Tranquebar, India

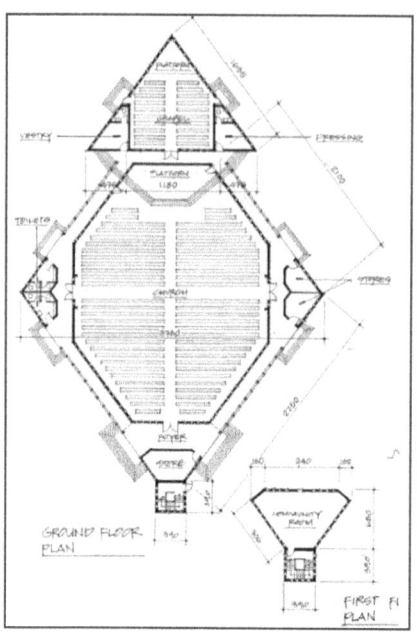

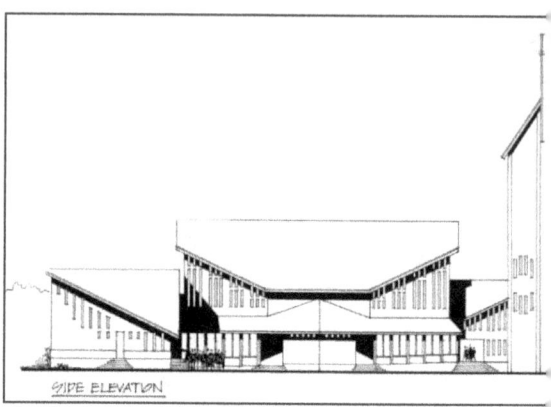

University Church in Maiduguri, Nigeria

Lutheran Church in 67 Ha Section of Antananarivo, Madagascar

Multi-Purpose Training Centre in Udaipur, Rajasthan, India

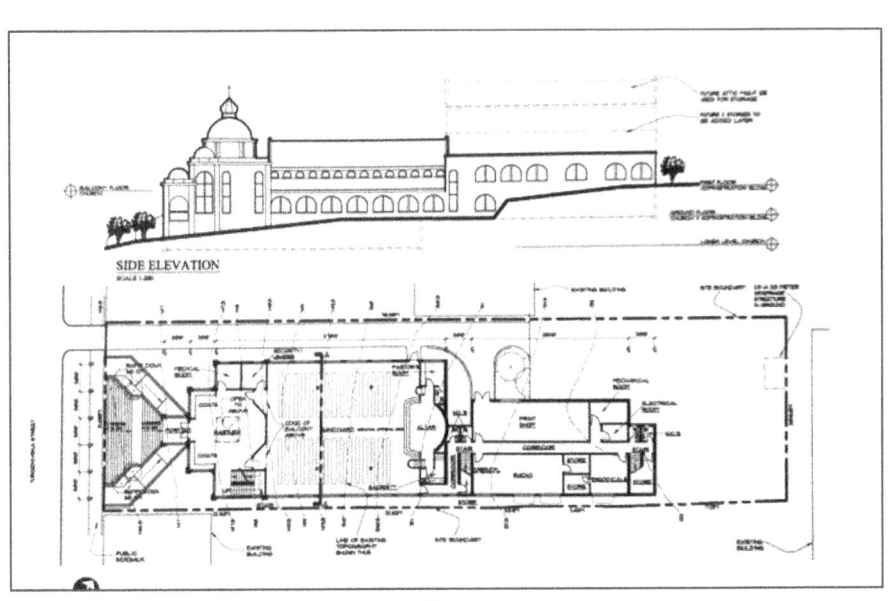

Proposed Lutheran Church in Kyiv, Ukraine

St. Francois des Sales University Hospital in Port-au-Prince, Haiti

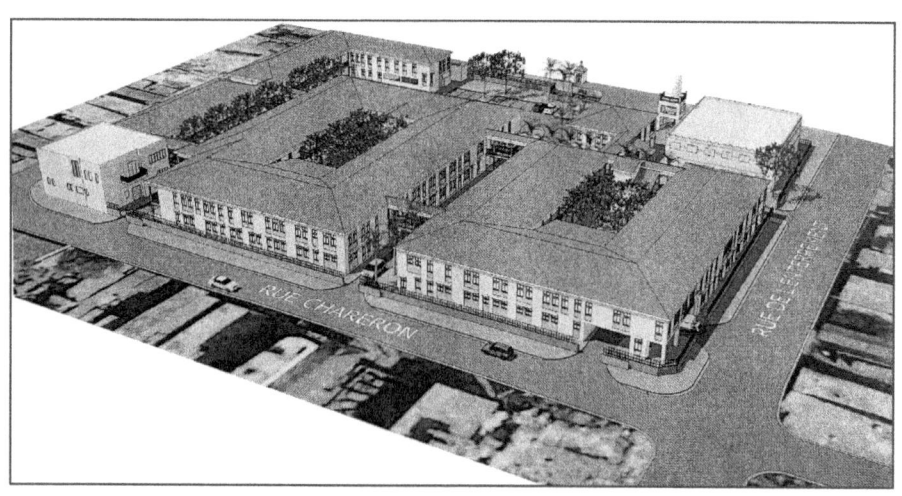

Roman Catholic Church in a suburb of Nairobi, Kenya

This wall was later decorated with a relevant crucifixion painting by a local artist.

Jebavidu at Siloam Girls' Boarding School, India

The 4,000-student school in Tiruvannamalai, India in the ALCSP

Arcot Lutheran Church School Project (ALCSP) in Tamil Nadu, India

One of the over one thousand classrooms built in the ALC School Project in India.

Chapel in the Lutheran Seminary project in Almaty, Kazakhstan

CHAPTER 4

TRULY SERVING TO MEET NEEDS

W orking in a wide range of countries for so many years has taught me how important it is for us architects to adapt and serve elsewhere in different ways than we might be used to in our home countries. This has led me to what has become my simple **"101 rule"** for being culturally sensitive: **"My way of doing things is not always the best.**"

Understanding that is what I was introduced to during the little over a year, I was a missionary architect in Nigeria and, later, during my six years in Tanzania. This rule was further reinforced for me during the many productive years after Msaada was founded.

Customs, Traditions, and Languages
Truly responsive architecture should respect the dignity of the people to be served by a new facility, and thus, design work should begin with an understanding of the customs and traditions of a specific community as well as of the broader culture in which a building is to be located. While the importance of being sensitive to the culture was made clear to me already in Nigeria, I learned it was also of great value to speak some of the local language during my time in Tanzania. As I was only to stay for a short time in Nigeria, it did not seem worthwhile to try speaking

the local language, and the Lutheran Church of Christ in Nigeria (LCCN) wasn't as indigenized, as I learned later that the Evangelical Lutheran Church in Tanzania (ELCT) was.

So, while I lived in Nigeria, I focused on speaking English, which was also a definite foreign language for me at that time. Further, it was the language spoken among the various Western missionaries who were there. It was also the language, after tribal languages and Hausa in Northern Nigeria, used by indigenous church leaders.

In Tanzania, my wife and I started out with a couple of months of orientation and language (Swahili) course, together with other Lutheran missionaries from different Western countries who were new to Tanzania. That course was mostly geared towards people who spoke English as their mother tongue, and it was, thus, more challenging for those of us who did not have that native language. Everything the U.S. missionary teacher explained about Swahili was based on how it compared to English.

Almost immediately after I had started working in the national central office of the ELCT, I realized though, how I was now in a country and serving in a church where the Africans were in charge, not the missionaries, as had been the case largely in Nigeria. Since I also became head of a department, I was expected to be part of some national committees and to attend heads-of-department meetings in the central office.

In an early committee meeting with one of the bishops of the ELCT, Rt. Rev. J. Kibera, as the committee chair, I started speaking in English. But Bishop Kibera quickly told me how I should understand that I now was in Tanzania, where Kiswahili — as it is called locally — is the national language. I am thankful, though, that the administrative head of the ELCT was Joel Ngeiyamu. He was, as General Secretary, tolerant of me, mostly speaking English, the second language in Tanzania.

Further, the A/E department prepared drawings and specifications in English, as this was what the building contractors expected. It was also what was required to get building permits approved in cities and towns. There are many things, though, that I would not have understood regarding projects outside the bigger cities and towns if I had not had at least a passable understanding of Swahili. This was also of great value to me later, as Msaada has done more projects in Tanzania than in any other country.

I therefore strongly support learning the local language when living or serving in another country for a longer period. I do this even as somebody who does not particularly enjoy the actual learning of new languages and who is not that good at it either.

Being a Catalyst for Projects

In Tanzania, I also learned to be a catalyst for new projects by learning what funding assistance was possible to obtain from the Lutheran World Foundation or directly from ELCT's partner churches in the Western world. More than a dozen of these were in different Western countries, which traditionally had served in various parts of Tanzania.

It was also essential that the projects for which funding was being sought fit with the priorities of the ELCT, that they were what was truly needed in Tanzania, and that they were what the local people desired. Only then could the humanitarian needs truly be met. However, it was a challenge to find a balance between all these factors to secure funding for projects in the developing world. Fortunately, the General Secretary of the ELCT willingly let me bounce responses to such challenges off him.

After having ensured that projects met these criteria — and still had attractive, functional designs and reasonable expected costs — we were all excited when projects obtained the required funding and even more thrilled when their construction was completed. This was because everybody could now celebrate together what the projects might mean for the people whose lives would be enhanced by the services that would be provided there.

Understanding not only the language but, even more so, the culture where you work and serve also helps you be a better catalyst as the A/E on building projects. While Msaada Architects has often had that role between the local client and an outside project donor, we have also tried to be a bridge between those in a country who feel more developed and those they feel are not.

An example of that was when a building contractor in India had done a school project in his home city of Madras (now called Chennai), with Msaada serving as the A/E. He requested a chance to do a project elsewhere. Thus, he got another school project to do in what was still a larger town, only for me to realize when I visited the project site that he was not doing the work well enough. When he excused this by saying he could not work properly among "such unsophisticated neighbors," I had the peculiar experience as a foreigner telling him that those people were his fellow citizens and that their children were the ones for whom Msaada Architects were there to help get a better school.

Ensure You are Meeting Needs

For me, a good example of how Msaada Architects has tried to be culturally sensitive when doing projects in developing countries includes designing some churches with the pastor being surrounded by the assembly instead of being isolated at one end of a rectangle (or a cross-shaped space). Such an approach to church design also relates better to the role of pastors — and especially bishops — who, as I have experienced it, seemingly often are seen as a substitute for tribal chiefs.

A new **Christ Church at Sevamandir in India** at a female boarding school with about 2,000 students is a good example of doing something different. The church was designed by the long-term Chief of Studio Architect in Msaada's home office, Scott Williams. It was based on a need to be attractive but not too dominant. The overarching design objective was for the church to relate respectfully to and not overpower the original building at Sevamandir, which was located right next to it. The "Father of India" (Mahatma Gandhi) had laid the cornerstone for that original building in the 1920s.

Although Scott literally did the initial design concept for that church on a napkin, that concept continued to guide the ensuing planning and design phases. Further, its pagoda shape allowed for a space to seat all 2,000 female students on the floor and still have a rather low exterior wall along which teachers and other staff were seated. The interior space rose to quite a high point appropriate for such a large space of worship.

But it is interesting how I periodically have been asked by Indian pastors when it might have become a practice to have pagoda shaped churches. Something which I usually replied to with that while that might not have been common to use that shape for church designs, it was a solution which as Scott realized, when he proposed it on a simple napkin, did fit this project extremely well as already explained above.

Further note that when the church was completed and inaugurated, Msaada received a letter from the head of Sevamandir, which included this excerpt: **"The church building has come up very nicely, and every detail is being studied. It stands very beautifully, and I can't find words to describe it. On the nights with all the lights on, it is simply beautiful. Whenever we sit for prayers in the beautiful church, MSAADA's name will be remembered. And the more we use the church, the more beautiful it seems to become."**

Ankaramalaza Lutheran Church in Madagascar was designed to meet the need for a smaller permanent space where church services could be held every Sunday. It was also designed so seating capacity could be dramatically expanded three to four times each year when large church services are held as part of a "Shepherd Program." While the local congregation wanted a church large enough to accommodate all these needs, during my visit to the project location — rather far from major roads and highways — I suggested building a smaller permanent building for most Sundays and then incorporating a tent structure into the design using the church tower as a "tent pole" when more space was required. This design solution was affordable within available funding.

So, although the local client, as well as the Western donor, thought they would get a church with the capacity to seat the enlarged congregation only a few times a year, Msaada's design enabled them to obtain what they needed. I was initially surprised, though, that such an unusual design solution was accepted, and when I brought the design concept back to Minnesota, Scott Williams made it both functional and feasible.

Another useful reference is a project to repair and renovate **Phebe Lutheran Hospital in Liberia** after a civil war. I thought the local client would never want to see me (or Msaada Architects) again after I had told our expat Clerk of Works to follow my instructions and not those of the local Medical Director, who wanted us to stop construction, in order to do some design changes that would have significantly delayed the project. I felt very bad about doing so, but I did it to ensure the project was completed in time, which was required for the donor to provide all the required funding. Later, when the hospital's Medical Director became Liberia's Minister of Health and Social Services, Msaada was, to my pleasant surprise, invited to work also on projects for that Government Ministry.

Some Personal Reflections

I want to add to this chapter some reflections, which I hope the readers will find relevant to living and serving in a country that is not your own, even though they are largely reflections of a more personal nature for me. Thus, let me first add how I often in Tanzania have come close to feeling almost like I belonged there.

This is different from India, even though I have always been treated extremely well there, too. But there have been numerous times when I have sat in meetings in India and felt how difficult it was for me to understand the Indians and their culture. This might also be because I never learned any Indian languages, although quite some time ago, I realized I had visited there well over 100 times on two-to-five-week working visits.

By comparison, shortly after Msaada Architects was founded, I returned to Tanzania primarily because of our first project, which was an **Extension of Makiungu Roman Catholic Hospital in Tanzania.** However, the Christian Council of Tanzania then asked me to also make a presentation about Msaada's services to all Tanzanian Protestant Bishops and General Secretaries in the national churches as well as in the various units of those churches. When doing that, I remember realizing, to my surprise, how I apparently was the only non-African in the auditorium. And I felt very much at home!

I am also aware, as stated earlier, that when working or serving in the developing world as a Westerner, you should never claim to understand everything about the country you are in. I have noted the negative reactions when some Westerners in developing countries have tried this. Instead, I believe one should remain ready to learn and grow in understanding a given country and its culture.

Related to that when my wife and I lived in Tanzania, conversations among us expats often turned to how we had met Westerners who, after visiting that country for a fortnight or so, did talk as if they now knew almost everything about Tanzania. Our experiences were that when you live for a longer time in a new country, you might feel, after maybe half a year, that you really don't know much at all. Then, maybe another half a year later, you begin to feel that you are starting to understand the country you are now in.

Similarly, I might mention that when I am asked what I feel about the U.S., I usually respond with something I have heard said and which I have come to believe, namely that "**you never truly leave your own country, but instead you take it with you in values and in many other ways**." For me, that relates also to the fact that I didn't leave Denmark because I was dissatisfied with my country. On the contrary, I am therefore usually also ready to promote Scandinavian (or Nordic) values in the U.S. because, for me, they seem to extensively agree with Christian values (as I understand these).

But I hurry to add that although I have kept my Danish citizenship, I consider myself primarily a global citizen. Something which I began realizing during my time of living Nigeria and Tanzania and something which has only been reinforced during the many years I later have served on projects in the developing world with the residence of my family and I in Minnesota. And while the three Scandinavian countries — Sweden, Denmark, and Norway — or the five Nordic countries, which also include Finland and Iceland, are often in the U.S. called "socialist countries," I believe that label is inaccurate. Instead, these countries might — as I have seen suggested somewhere — be called "**social investment countries,**" which blends the best of capitalism with the best of socialism.

A blending which has resulted in that there are not many countries in the world which have more equality financially in its population than the Nordic countries. This also means there isn't the same need in those countries for what I as a Scandinavian see as a too excessive system of "donation begging" by too many organizations in the U.S. trying to do what in a rich democratic country as this one – again as I see it as a Scandinavian — should be the responsibility morally and otherwise of the federal or state governments.

Religious or Spiritual Reflections

The previous comment gives me an opportunity to express also, how I much appreciate having grown up in Denmark and I have further come to realize how I was richly blessed by living and serving national Lutheran churches in Nigeria and Tanzania as a missionary architect, as that led to the founding of Msaada Architects. For managing this global humanitarian design organization has allowed me to continue letting **"my life speak the values I have come to believe in"**, as I recall having heard it expressed.

By doing so, I have learned that wanting to live a meaningful life that matters often involves conflicts between following your better conscience instead of what others might consider as being successful. I have also learned to recognize this as being a natural part of wanting to be a humble Christian and an egalitarian, which for me is what I attempt to be first as a human being and secondly as an architect.

Related to that, I have often returned to what my wife Susanna has reminded me about periodically, namely that before she and I married, a close friend of hers, who was a Roman Catholic nun, suggested to her that I was **"listening to the beat of a different drum."** A description which I hope I have been able to live up to. So, after I initially was very reluctant to become a missionary architect, I later realized, to my definite surprise, how listening to the beat of that different drum led me to a lifelong vocation. Something which also required a personal faith transformation, leading me further in getting a different understanding of God and religion than what I had grown up with in Denmark in a family with a strong pietistic approach to Christianity.

So, through having been involved in serving together with fellow Christians of many different denominations and cultures in Africa and other parts of the world — in whatever role we all have been allowed to play in the "Great Commission" — I have ended up with what I believe is a more Gospel oriented Christian faith. That is compared to what I was exposed to in my family during my upbringing, but it is still in line with what is practiced in my home country within what is often called the Lutheran "Folkekirke" (**Folk Church).**

I know there are many in the U.S. who question the organized Lutheran churches in the Scandinavian (or Nordic) countries and, thus, also what being a Folk Church really means. This has often been difficult for me to explain to Americans. However, it has become easier recently, when many in the Western world are maybe not losing their faith in God, but instead losing their faith in the organized church that was supposed to help us truly grasp God. For I believe the Folk Church in my home country has reacted well to that by focusing more on living out Christan values, and therefore also suggesting we should live as Christ taught us through his own life on this earth more than talking about or preaching verbally what faith in the triune God means or does require of us.

I therefore found it both relevant and uplifting when I recently read an article in a major Danish national newspaper with a rather long heading which in English translates into: **"Maybe we are trying to convince** ourselves that we have moved on from Christianity, but we have not. Instead, Christianity is the truth about us."

That is something I personally agree with, and I also believe it describes Denmark and its Folk Church very well — plus likely also the four other Nordic countries. And I do so, although one can then maybe argue Christianity has become more cultural than faith based, as such a situation emphasizes living out Christian values more than having an actual faith in Jesus the Christ, which naturally is of great importance spiritually. Although it might also involve a redefining of faith, at least as opposed to how I have traditionally understood it. In that connection, it is interesting also how the 19th century highly influential Danish pastor, educator, and hymn writer N. F. S. Grundtvig did once suggest something like "**Humanity first, then Religion.**"

That statement seems to be relevant to most Danes even today, after Denmark was introduced to Christianity more than 1,000 years ago in the Viking Age. For recent statistics confirm that about 75% of all Danes are members of the Folk Church and thus also pay the taxes required to operate that church. Those statistics also show how more than half of all Danes use the Folk Church annually, mostly for baptisms, confirmations, weddings, or funerals, while only about 14% attend at least one normal church service annually. The latter is despite that close to half of all Danes indicate they have a Christian faith, or that they treasure Christianity as a valuable cultural inheritance.

But back to how I left my home country because I believe life should be experienced and not just lived. I have seen that described as finding the right balance between what is possible and what is necessary. Something which is affected also by an individual's potential skills and age etc., I didn't know, though, how my leaving Denmark would be for good, although I believe, as the Danish author Hans Christian Andersen often stressed, that "**to travel is to live.**" So, I have been blessed with a richer and wider range of experiences — both professionally and personally — than I likely would have had if I had lived and worked my entire professional life in my home country as an architect.

For me very Surprising Information

I will close this chapter by sharing what I was shocked to learn about rather recently, when I first heard about the centuries old **Doctrine of Discovery.** A doctrine, which was used originally to justify politically and morally the colonization and consequent exploitation by the European countries of the indigenous populations in other parts of the world. It was also used in the U.S. to similarly justify exploiting Native Americans as well as the many slaves who were brought from Africa against their own will.

All something which — at least as I see it — is not in line with a true understanding of Christianity. This is maybe, therefore, something which persons in the Western world — including the organized Western Church denominations themselves — are simply uncomfortable talking about or accepting as part of world history for about 500 years. Although exploitation of indigenous people is still practiced extensively in the developing world not only by Western and other governments including recently in Africa especially by the Chinese government. But in recent years also by large business corporations, which include not least many mining corporations.

Christ Church at Sevamandir, India

Scott Wiliam's concept design on a simple napkin

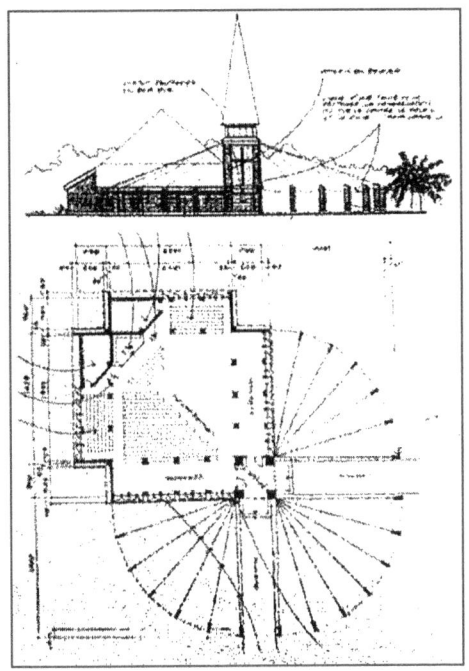

Ankaramalaza Lutheran Church in Madagascar

PART TWO

UNIQUE AS
MASTER BUILDER

CHAPTER 5

SERVING CHURCH-SPONSORED PROJECTS

It has often been affirmed how Msaada Architects seemingly found the right niche for serving in the developing world by concentrating on doing so as a Master Builder on projects for Christian churches, missions, and related organizations. Since this focus initially was based largely on my experiences as a missionary architect in Nigeria and Tanzania, I now appreciate how my successors as Executive Director should also share the Christian values upon which the organization was founded.

Msaada Architects' Vision
Experiences throughout Msaada Architects' history have repeatedly reinforced the value of our emphasis on serving on church-sponsored projects. Haiti provides a rather recent example of this, for while a lot of funds were promised for government projects in Haiti by the Western countries after the 2010 earthquake, a significant portion of those funds are still held up. In contrast, since that major natural disaster, Msaada has been fortunate to work on numerous projects in Haiti for churches, missions, and other NGOs and has further been blessed to see most of those efforts result in implemented projects.

A prime example of such a project is the initial large, substantial one that Msaada Architects completed in Haiti after the earthquake. This was the **Healing Hands for Haiti (HHH) Physical Rehabilitation Center in Port-au-Prince**, which, at the time of its construction, attracted a great deal of attention from others working in Haiti. That was because the project was completed quite quickly and without compromising high-quality construction. Something which was required by the client (HHH) as well as by the project donor, the International Committee of the Red Cross (ICRC), and by us in Msaada.

Thus, when the construction of that project was completed, we were glad to receive a message that included these words from the Board Chair of the HHH at that time: **"I want to thank you again for the beautiful ICRC building. I was told by the ICRC that you did a terrific job throughout the entire project, that your plans were superlative, and that they would highly recommend you. I was extremely impressed with the building when I finally got to see it at the opening ceremony."**

As a relevant side note, it is unfortunate, though, how Haiti has experienced so many serious problems over the last few years. As I see it, this relates to how much development in Haiti should have been handled much better — both nationally and internationally — to have helped prevent the present political chaos in that country. The local population already has been through so much, and, thus, does not deserve the now so complicated situation they are currently enduring.

However, a possible positive outcome from the present challenges in Haiti could be that the international community now might truly assist the country, not in deciding how it should be, but instead allowing Haitians to make their own decisions about the future of their country. First France, as the former colonial power, and then the U.S. have influenced the development of Haiti in both positive and negative ways. The latter does for the U.S. relate also to how large numbers of Americans have traveled there in recent years for short-term visits believing they were helping the country, but they have instead been part of creating dependency, which has prevented capacity building of the local population.

Founding Msaada Architects and Getting it Up and Running

Msaada Architects was founded after several non-Lutheran churches and missions in Tanzania had requested A/E services when I was heading up the Evangelical Lutheran Church in Tanzania (ELCT) A/E Department. Other European architects and building engineers with a background like mine of having served and lived in Africa for some years had "diagnosed" identical needs on that continent. They had, however, not been able to meet those needs because they started out believing that doing so would require part (or most) of the operating budget for such an A/E service organization to come from Western donations and/or grants. They failed to locate anybody ready to provide such funding, as I was informed by the Lutheran World Foundation (LWF).

Knowing this made it extra challenging to get Msaada Architects off the ground, since the organization set out with the clear objective of achieving self-sufficiency rather quickly by being paid fees for services that would cover operating expenses. It was also important to promptly repay an interest-free loan from my two co-founders of the organization, which had been required and used to get it off the ground financially.

Achieving these objectives, I felt, should be possible based on my experience heading up the A/E Department in the ELCT central office in Tanzania. This is because, after the first couple of years, we were, in that department, able to cover operating expenses from the limited fees received on projects served, apart from the compensation paid from other sources for expat staff, which included me, as a Western missionary, plus a Danish volunteer architect or engineer off and on.

Two factors made that arrangement desirable and feasible. First, it seems that something provided without any cost to the recipient of a project is not nearly as appreciated as something paid for with even a small fee. Further, when implementing the first project for the ELCT A/E Department, which was a new, very large **Lutheran Junior Seminary in Morogoro, Tanzania,** we were able to show how construction cost savings covered at least the fees we were paid for our professional A/E services.

Those savings were realized due to the functionality and efficiency of project designs and during construction because local skilled craftsmen could complete their work less expensively when employed as brand-new building contractors. This situation will be explained further later. We also paid advances on the new contractors' contracts. I thus believed the same approach could be effectively used by Msaada, which fortunately proved at least to be mostly correct.

Note also how I have never been bashful about seeking funding for a required project to be done in the developing world for a church with support, often from a Western mission. But I am very uncomfortable about asking for funds to pay for my own salary. I was thus glad — as a missionary in Nigeria and Tanzania — that I was paid a low but steady salary. This is different from the practice of many U.S. missionaries who, as I understand it, must often collect fully or partly their own compensation during home furloughs.

When Msaada Architects has had expatriates serving in our overseas offices, we have, therefore, always paid them salaries, although those have been lower than comparable U.S. salaries. The same has also been applied to architects and other staff serving in the Minnesota home office. I thus believe a major reason Msaada has been blessed to see as many projects implemented as we have in the developing world includes how everybody working for us has had to work efficiently and diligently for their salaries.

Founding Msaada Architects also provided a way for me to fulfill the desire I had developed to use my profession to live out the "Great Commission." It has also been great to have had many people of the Christian faith working for Msaada Architects. We have also had employees, though, who stated before accepting a position that they did not consider themselves Christians, but they would like to be involved with our work.

We usually agreed to hire them if they were qualified to do what was expected of them professionally, and if they convincingly shared how they were ready to work mostly with churches and missions and understood they would have to deal respectfully with clergy and other committed Christian leaders.

As an example for that, the first Danish volunteer we had serving in the A/E department of the ELCT central office was a structural engineer who was not a member of any church in Denmark. This person served extremely well on projects and was both respected and appreciated by the Tanzanians.

I have tended to think of such persons as "secular Christians," and some of those working for Msaada proved to be among the best staff we have had. I admire this as I know it would have been difficult — or likely impossible — for me to personally have spent about five decades serving in or for the developing world if it had not been because of my firm belief that being called a Christian believer require me to accept financial sacrifices also, to truly live out, to the best of my ability what I understand as authentic Christian values.

Serving as a Nonprofit Based on Fees Received
As mentioned already, during the six years the ELCT A/E Department in Tanzania was developed, I learned how people generally don't seem to value what they receive for free as much as what they have at least partially paid for. While I was a missionary in charge of that department, I received a modest compensation from Denmark and so did the volunteers, who were sent to work with us a few times by a secular Danish organization.

Thus, we were able to make the A/E Department the first financially self-sufficient department in the ELCT central office. That was accomplished by charging the various synods and dioceses fees for the services provided. And although those fees were low, they were sufficient to pay fair and reasonable salaries to our local staff, plus they covered other required operating expenses.

This experience, therefore, reinforced to me the idea that Msaada Architects could be founded based on the idea of receiving limited fees compared to what other Western firms might charge for providing professional A/E services in the developing world. Doing so on a non-profit basis helped to ensure that fees charged could be as low as possible.

We got a surprise, though, when we initially were to incorporate Msaada Architects as a nonprofit organization in Minnesota and learned how (at that time) it was not possible to do this here, if we wanted to operate entirely based on fees charged for services provided. This was possible in other states, though, such as in California, which I had learned about, even before Susanna and I and our family moved to Minnesota, after we had completed our missionary services in the national Lutheran Church in Tanzania.

So, Msaada Architects was originally incorporated as something else, although we operated on a not-for-profit basis. And later, when it became possible to also be officially in Minnesota what Msaada Architects had already been in practice — a corporation operating on a non-profit basis based on received fees only — the organization became at the outset of 1997 an incorporated Chapter 317A nonprofit corporation under the Minnesota Statues.

We thus also got a 501©3 status, which meant we could receive donations that were tax deductible for the persons giving them. This has been helpful for covering part of our operating expenses for short periods of time during transitions. However, I have always understood that a nonprofit — besides not providing any profit to share — should still operate as frugally as possible.

But the understanding here in the U.S. seems to focus often on how nonprofits can plan on receiving donations for covering part of the operating expenses that are tax-free gifts for the financial donors. That is different from a main original Msaada objective which was that we should serve based on the local level A/E fees received, although those are usually a good deal lower in the developing world than in the Western world.

There are also Western A/E firms which offer to work pro bono in the developing world. That often results, though, in designs that are not relevant to their locations. And while there now are both commercial firms and other Western nonprofits serving on building projects in the developing world, I have yet to learn about another nonprofit A/E firm or organization that works as Msaada Architects traditionally did for most of its years, with operating expenses usually being fully covered by local-level A/E fees.

Instead, other Western nonprofit A/E organizations seem to have either a sizeable part of operation expenses covered by grants and/or donations, or they rely on using volunteers who are not sufficiently familiar with the cultures to be served, which often results in designs that are too expensive to build or are, in other ways, inappropriate.

Such trends are part of what prompted me to write this book. The timing also seems good, because in its initial years, Msaada could attract the best new architectural graduates to work for the organization. But this situation changed in the new millennium, so it was no longer as easy to recruit staff willing to produce "**more than average work for less than average salaries.**" For I personally believe doing the kind of work Msaada does requires economic sacrifices and that these are balanced by the intrinsic and lasting rewards of doing something meaningful, plus the opportunity to live an interesting life. As the poet Robert Bly has pointed out, the goal in life should not be to **"end up with a lot of stuff and an empty life!"**

It has thus been good to observe how many of today's young people now again realize the value of doing something meaningful for others, even if it provides less financial compensation. I have recently heard this described as **"giving forward,"** in contrast to **"giving back,"** which is so common in this country. I have thus also realized that "giving forward" is what I did as a young architect going initially to Nigeria and what I have practiced since then without earlier having had a well-known term to use for that.

So, by presenting now what others and I have learned by working in the developing world for decades, I hope architectural students and architects will identify meaningful ways in which they can by "giving forward" apply their knowledge, passion, and skills to designing and implementing facilities that meet basic human needs in the developing world with truly responsive architecture — and maybe elsewhere, too.

I have often reflected on how my wife Susanna has often said — when she and I have talked about financial matters — that while we as a family maybe never have had too much financially, God has faithfully ensured that we always have had enough. And by living frugally, we have also realized the true value of the anonymous saying, which so wisely suggests that **"when you love what you have you have everything you need."**

Keeping Msaada Architects Operating

A major logistic reason why Msaada Architects has been able to see accomplished what we have of church-sponsored building projects in the developing world stems from our willingness to assume the risk of providing preliminary planning and design services with reliable cost estimates for good projects initiated by indigenous churches. We have usually only been paid for those services if a project eventually did receive funding. And although I don't have specific data regarding this system to refer to, I believe that without it, most of the projects Msaada Architects has served on and been blessed to see implemented in the developing world might not have materialized. This system's success has further depended on the fact that at least half of the projects initiated that way had to eventually get funded to make it financially feasible for us to assist in this way.

But it has thus also provided a strong incentive for Msaada to only work on projects that we believe can be funded and not on those likely to end up as only "paper architecture." For while such paper architecture might help, for example, design organizations and university students grow professionally and academically — as has been realized by many U.S. universities that have sent architectural students to developing countries for a short time — such arrangements can create tremendous disappointment for the community a suggested new facility would have served, if it does not get implemented.

Thus, far too often, I have seen people in the developing world realize with great disappointment that what they thought was being planned and designed for them by organizations or university students coming to their country for a short period of time will never become more than attractive drawings that do nothing to enhance their lives.

In recent years, more architects from the Western world have begun pursuing Humanitarian or Public Interest Design work in the developing world, too. This means Msaada Architects has had to not only compete so to speak with local architects and engineers, who often suggest fees and construction costs can be lower than what is realistic, but also with other Western architects and engineers working on a nonprofit basis, but with them having operational expenses covered largely by donations and grants. This is in addition to those from the Western world serving in the developing world on a pro bono basis, with designs that often end up not being culturally relevant.

Msaada Architects' services, therefore, as I see it, have traditionally crossed the boundaries between different categories of A/E organizations working in the developing world. But to sustain the model for serving in the future as an important, still-needed ministry for projects in the developing world, the organization has now begun supplementing its fee income with grants and/or donations. Thus, it will likely also arrange financial matters in a different way than was the case in the initial four decades of the organization's existence when I was the Executive Director.

While those are changes that I would not have been able to make in the services provided by Msaada Architects — at least based on the original idea of what Msaada Architects should be — I realize the need now for me to accept that the organization's present leadership believes such changes are required for them to continue to serve churches, missions and related organizations in the developing world.

And I do so even though that brings Msaada closer to what other U.S. organizations are doing in the developing world instead of breaking new ground for how to serve church-sponsored projects in that part of the world. Note also, though, that when Msaada served primarily on projects funded by European church-related donor organizations in the 1980s and 1990s, that is different from today when most of the church-sponsored projects the organization is involved with are funded here from the U.S. Thus, the organization likely also should be more Americanized for lack of a better term.

I realize that some might not be comfortable with me using such a term. But it is something I do naturally as a product of having grown up in Scandinavia. So, I do not use it as a negative term, but simply to state how there are many differences between the way smaller Northern European countries can assist with development challenges in the developing world compared to how the much larger, more complex U.S. does so.

Likewise, I have also realized from having served for over four decades in the developing world through Msaada Architects having its home office in Minnesota, how Americans are usually quite comfortable with talking about themselves and what they might be capable of doing. But I come from a culture in Scandinavia where we prefer to let others express what they believe we might be capable of doing.

However, irrespective of what led to Msaada Architects being located in Minnesota, that state has been good for Susanna and me and our children. So, I believe, that I did right by keeping focused on what I have done for most of my professional life from a home base in Minnesota, although I started out by serving our global neighbors through Christian mission organizations in my home country. Because whatever I otherwise might have done for 50+ years as an architect, I would likely not have had the same feeling of hopefully having lived a **meaningful life that mattered**, as I recall having heard it expressed so well by the Jewish Rabbi Harold S. Kushner.

Let me also mention how Msaada earlier did not have written contracts with the mostly Northern European funding organizations for projects implemented for and by their partner churches in the developing world. That changed, though, when we in the new millennium shifted to serving mostly on projects funded from the U.S. We then used a Memorandum of Agreement based on one developed by the Royal Institute of British Architects (RIBA) because the long The American Institute of Architects (AIA) contract forms cover so much more than what needs to be included for projects in the developing world.

We realized this primarily when some U.S. clients demanded we use AIA contract forms. This resulted in added project costs, especially when such forms were used for contracts between the clients and the building contractors. For the latter included extra costs to cover unforeseen or unexpected expenses in tenders/bids because of their concern about things that might happen in a U.S. setting but would most likely not occur in other parts of the world. But it is now up to my successors as Executive Director, presently and in the future to decide which contract forms Msaada Architects will use.

HHH Physical Rehab Centre in Port-au-Prince, Haiti

Lutheran Junior Seminary in Morogoro, Tanzania

Classroom Buildings

Dormitory Units

CHAPTER 6

MSAADA ARCHITECTS' ACTIVITIES

Although I was doing projects as an architect in the developing world before Msaada Architects was founded in 1980, this chapter will focus on project activities by that organization during the approximately four decades I was the Executive Director. **The world map** shows the countries where Msaada has been involved.

Projects for Whom and Where

Most of the projects that Msaada has been involved with in close to 50 countries worldwide have, as mentioned already, been for Christian churches, missions, or related organizations in mostly the developing world. These include over a dozen Christian church denominations and about 60 Christian missions or church-related organizations in the Western world, such as the YMCA, the YWCA, World Vision, and Mission Aviation Fellowship, to mention just a few.

In some special situations, Msaada Architects has also worked for Western government aid organizations that assist in the developing world. These have been limited to mostly being from the U.S. or from the three Scandinavian countries. In Tanzania and Madagascar, Msaada has also served a couple of national park agencies and the Western organizations supporting them, such as the Frankfurt Zoological Society from Germany. Msaada has also served a few secular organizations in both the Western World and in Africa, with the latter including, for example, the Mwalimu Nyerere Foundation in Tanzania and a government ministry in Liberia.

Tanzania and India are the countries where most of the close to 1,000 projects, which Msaada Architects has so far seen implemented, are located, followed by Madagascar and Kenya. There are also several developing countries where Msaada was asked to serve, but where no envisioned projects ever materialized for a variety of reasons.

Some of the projects that weren't implemented were ones Msaada agreed to work on in the Western world based on special requests from organizations it already had served in the developing world. These mostly include a few projects in Europe and in the Far East, but also some in the U.S. — although most of the special-request projects in the U.S. were built. It is also part of Msaada's original vision as a Christian ministry to respond to what is truly needed. Thus, the organization has usually prioritized projects that possibly might not materialize without its assistance. For only then has Msaada stayed a true non-profit A/E service organization.

However, in addition to meeting this rather ambitious objective, it has been a great pleasure for my co-workers and I in Msaada Architects to have also realized the value of what an instructor at the well-known

Bauhaus University in Germany said approximately a century ago: **"Our play should become work; and our celebration, play,"** after which, he added, **"I regard this as the supreme excellence of human tasks."**

It seems relevant to add to this, how when some people in the U.S. have periodically asked me — seemingly with sincere concern — whether Msaada is ready to serve in all countries in the developing world irrespective of their political leaning, my answer has always been a clear "yes," and I usually then have added, how Msaada **serves people, not the countries they live in**!

Appropriate Development and Growth

Msaada Architects' priority has further been to serve on projects that are truly needed and wanted by the country where they are located because it is essential that the people who live in a country determine what these projects should be rather than Western donors deciding what they might desire to "give." The latter has, too often, been the case on projects in the developing world funded with assistance from the Western world.

Related to that, when I was living and working as a missionary architect in Tanzania for six years in the 1970s, I was greatly inspired by the former President of Tanzania, the now late Dr. Julius Nyerere, who so eloquently stated: **"Developments are to be about the human being and NOT about the tools of development, such as buildings, roads and other physical infrastructures."**

I wholeheartedly agree with this philosophy. It has shaped the vision and mission of Msaada Architects throughout the organization's history. More specifically, Dr. Julius Nyerere, who was also called "Mwalimu," ("teacher" in Swahili) said: **"It is important that assistance from the Western world to the developing world is based on what is truly needed and not on misdirected intentions of those from the Western World, regardless how good and noble their intentions might be."**

So, as this book intends to illustrate, we in the Western world must prioritize flexibility and understanding over ideology and personal beliefs if we want to ensure that basic human needs are truly met in immediate and sustainable ways in the developing world.

This contradicts the opinion of many design professionals and others whom I have met in the developing world who have stated that they feel it is preferable for developing countries to emulate the Western world. Based on my experiences and observations, I feel nothing could be further from the truth. I also believe much of the tension in our world, between individuals, between people of different backgrounds, and between nations, is mostly a result of people not knowing enough about each other!

As the late African American author and pastor, Rev. Dr. Howard Thurman once stated: **"Any person is a human being, no more, no less. The awareness of this fact marks the supreme moment of human dignity."** Dr. Thurman, among many other things, was a spiritual mentor for Rev. Dr. Martin Luther King, Jr.

By listening deeply to the needs expressed by those who will inhabit, use, and visit a building — as well as those who are providing the funds — and addressing these needs with appropriate architectural designs, you can honor our shared humanity and treat all involved with dignity.

Surely, anything that increases mutual understanding and respect between people throughout the world can also help to reduce wars and other conflicts. However, I am certainly not an expert on that. Instead, I will again refer to the wisdom of the first President of Tanzania, Dr. Julius Nyerere, who was often referred to as the "conscience," of Africa and who once stated this also: **"We the people of Tanzania, would like to light a candle and put it on the top of Mt. Kilimanjaro which would shine beyond our borders giving hope where there was despair, love where there was hate and dignity where before there was only humiliation…We cannot, like other countries, send rockets to** the moon, but we can send rockets of love and hope to all our fellow humans wherever they might be."

To follow up on those wise words, I will simply point out how I believe one can choose to play a positive role in imagining a better world together with our global neighbors and then play a tangible role in rendering it real with whatever opportunity.

As an architect, the better you understand that the way buildings are planned, designed, and implemented in the developing world will affect people's everyday lives, the better you will be able to optimize investments provided by Western donors. This is what has continued to inspire me — and other staff in Msaada Architects — to create appropriate designs that are implemented for reasonable costs and with projected long lifespans.

This is no small task. It can, for example, be complicated and challenging to tell Western clients that they should listen more to the local clients regarding what is most important for a project — especially when the Western client team members are covering a major part of a project's cost. And while the Western clients need to listen to the local clients to ensure a building project will address the most critical needs and that the building can be properly operated and maintained over time, the local clients cannot expect more than what the Western project partner is willing (or able) to contribute financially.

Published About Msaada's Work
A 1989 article titled "Mud and Mortar," by Heather Beal, was the first article about Msaada Architects published in *Architecture, Minnesota.* Later, articles in that magazine included one with the title "African Cures," which highlighted the differences between medical projects in the U.S. and those Msaada Architects had completed in the developing world. Subsequently, another article that was simply titled "African Cure" focused on one of Msaada Architects' hospital designs in Tanzania. *Architecture Minnesota* also published an article describing the work we did to restore, the earlier mentioned 300-year-old Church of

Zion in Tranquebar, India, as well as "Madagascar Connection," an article by Scott Williams that profiled Msaada's work in that country.

Further, I was once invited to be one of six architects living and working in Minnesota who were asked to share our reflections about places around the world that had inspired us professionally in an *Architecture Minnesota* article titled "Forms of Inspiration." I chose the traditional African Hut as my example of inspiration. Scott Williams and I have also periodically contributed information to articles about Msaada's work in smaller and lesser-known architectural publications, such as for example, *Architectus.*

Msaada Architects' work has also been published in the *Journal of Interfaith Forum on Religion & Art*, *The Lutheran*, and the *ADA Magazine* in Denmark. One of the Danish articles had a headline that translates into English as "When Something Has to Be Created from Nothing." Another headline translates more straightforwardly as "Building of Churches in the Third World." That was because it was presented together with one titled "Building of Churches in Greenland,' which is part of the Kingdom of Denmark.

Additionally, Msaada has had articles about its work and the projects it has dealt with over the years published in various mission-related publications in the Western World and in several newspapers in the U.S. and in Scandinavia.

A few years ago, an interesting article appeared in a Danish American heritage journal, *The Bridge.* Written by Jens Vange, an architect of Danish descent who was working in Minneapolis, this article was especially meaningful for me because after the author explained how his parents were Danes who had immigrated to the U.S. and that he, therefore, made regular visits to Denmark as a child, he wrote the following:

"A significant impact on my design sensibilities has also been my exposure to Danish design, from the modern furniture in my childhood home to seeing new buildings in my visits to Denmark throughout my life. A few Danish firms and architects stood out to

me, the first being **MSAADA, which is a Minneapolis-based firm owned by Danish architect Poul Bertelsen. Most of their projects are in developing countries, and they focus on facilities that support their communities. It's an amazing model for bridging the world with much-needed expertise and resources.**"

I must clarify, though, that with Msaada Architects being a nonprofit organization, I have never actually owned the firm personally. However, Jens Vange's article then goes on to mention two other Danish architectural firms that he respects: Arne Jacobsen's and Bjarke Ingels' (who founded BIG). He then writes: "**These three firms, for me, embody Danish design principles that I feel should be universal — they are simple, practical, sustainable and therefore durable, and most importantly, humane. All of these shape how we experience the built world.**"

I agree with and much appreciate the final remark regarding design principles in my home country, especially the part about these being humane. However, I have never thought of myself as being in the league — for lack of a better team — of Arne Jacobsen and Bjarke Ingels.

Acknowledgements and Cooperations

As an egalitarian, I am not so big on awards, either. However, I appreciated accepting a "Special Award" from AIA Minnesota on behalf of Msaada in 2012 for **"dedication to international projects that provide better buildings and living conditions for people in distressed communities."**

In contrast, when the now late Peter Rand was the Executive Vice President of AIA Minnesota as well as Board Chair for Msaada Architects, he asked if, in his role as a Fellow of the American Institute of Architects (FAIA), he could recommend me for that designation. I respectfully declined his proposal, seemingly to his surprise.

I did so mostly because I believe that although I founded and then led Msaada Architects, I was aware that what had been accomplished could never have happened if I had not had such great coworkers. Those included Western building professionals, indigenous staff in area offices, and other associates of Msaada Architects throughout the developing world.

So why should I alone be recognized for what had been done in cooperation with my co-workers? For with reference to a very common saying, no architect is an island either. Rather, his or her ability to complete projects depends extensively on co-workers and associates, including building contractors and their crews.

For that reason, l also prefers using the terms "we" or "us" more than "I" and "me" when talking about Msaada Architects and the many projects which the organization has been richly blessed to serve on as an A/E nonprofit in so many countries worldwide.

Present and Future Msaada Architects

I appreciate that it is W. Jerry Murray who took over as Executive Director for Msaada Architects after my retirement, for the organization should, therefore, continue to be available to serve primarily in the developing world. I am further glad that Jerry's experiences include working for approximately a decade as the second staff person at Msaada, after me, and later working for three decades in the U.S. He was president of a commercial architecture firm for the last two of those decades. Jerry should, therefore, be well qualified to determine what can beneficially be applied to working and serving overseas today. As with any transition, there might now be changes from how Msaada served before to how it might do so now and in the future.

In the past, I have been told by several financial professionals here in the U.S. how there are ways in which Msaada was set up and worked for its initial four decades that should have made it impossible for us to survive from a traditional financial viewpoint in this country. But we did so anyway because God so generously blessed our efforts and maybe also because my wife and I have made financial sacrifices that goes beyond what can or should likely be expected by the Executive Director in the future.

Thus, to ensure future financial sustainability, I realize now how some changes are probably required for Msaada. This includes then also how earned fees might, as mentioned earlier, be somehow subsidized from grants and/or donations.

However, I trust that the tradition of the organization **working together with our global neighbors** more than serving on projects for them based primarily on directions from a Western mission or another donor organization will not be lost. Because I see that as an essential part of why we have been blessed to see so many projects materialize in the developing world for so long — despite us having had our own sizeable financial challenges to deal with. This is, though, very much like the situation for our clients in the developing world. So, we have had at least a bit of solidarity with them.

Generally, other U.S. nonprofit A/E firms or organizations now serving in the developing world are unable to operate entirely based on low-level local fees. While I earlier had appreciated and felt it important, when I led the organization, that it continued to serve based on only the rather low fees received for those services, I also realize as mentioned earlier how that was easier during the initial two decades of the organization's existence, when Msaada was primarily serving on European funded church-sponsored projects in the developing world.

In fact, it proved to be much more difficult after the initial two decades in the 21st century, when U.S.-based organizations provided funding for most of the projects Msaada served on. Further, the Msaada transition around the year 2000 could not have happened without operating expenses being supplemented with donated funds for a short time.

It is important also to stress how there was a considerable difference in serving on projects in the developing world being funded primarily by the larger church-related organizations, mostly in Northern Europe, which are all set up specifically to fund projects like that for their partner churches in primarily the developing world. For Msaada could then concentrate on providing the best possible and most economical A/E services within the limitation created by low fees.

That is different from when Msaada, in the new millennium, has served mostly on projects for individual church congregations as well as for smaller U.S. organizations, most of which have still been in the process of learning how to best assist in the developing world. That has often resulted in Msaada having had to provide services even further beyond what might, for lack of a better term, be called traditional A/E services.

Based also on these challenges, W. Jerry Murray, my immediate successor as Executive Director, has begun putting more emphasis on sharing through newsletters what the organization is doing in different countries, in mostly the developing world. That is something I can only support as part of recognizing the need for the organization to stay financially sustainable based on a different situation also from when the organization was initially founded in 1980.

I am saying this even though when, in the past, I periodically have mentioned to some people or organizations we have served, that we maybe should have shared more information about Msaada's work, and what it has meant for the people whose lives have been enhanced by the services they received in the new facilities built, I usually got the reply — including from board members of Msaada Architects — that it probably was better for us to continue concentrating on getting as many projects as possible done well, instead of talking more about or having articles or newsletters dealing with and showing what we were doing.

Often, they then would add, how they saw our attitude about that as a **"truly unique part of what Msaada Architects by that point had been offering for so many church-sponsored building projects in the developing world."** A response which I always have appreciated as a person who grew up in progressive Scandinavia with human equality demonstrated locally. This made it natural for me to eventually commit my work to making equality more available throughout parts of the world, irrespective of how enormous and complicated a task that seemingly might be.

For whatever we individually might be doing can only be like a drop of water. However, as often suggested by numerous other persons, we need to have many such drops before we can have a measurable amount of water, and there is no doubt — in my mind at least — that there is an urgent need for much more human equality in this world of ours. It is therefore very unfortunate how it still seems that racism may be more than politics provides the most toxic and painful limitation to experiencing true equality for so many of our fellow human beings worldwide.

CHAPTER 7

MARKETING AND GETTING COMMISSIONS

During my time as executive director, Msaada Architects served primarily on project initiated by indigenous churches or other local Christian organizations in the developing world. Thus, most new clients have in the past simply contacted us with a request to serve on their project. Or they have come to us via "word of mouth" referrals from former clients. This meant earlier there was not much need for marketing beyond continuing to do all our projects to the best of our abilities, as I always have believed that is the best marketing for doing anything, not least related to something as meaningful as what Msaada Architects has traditionally been doing.

The situation regarding the need for marketing has though changed some in recent years, as there now are more A/E non-profits in the U.S. wanting to serve in the developing world. If they serve in a way that ensures projects are done economically with appropriate designs and implemented with quality construction, then this is, of course, a positive development. For Msaada Architects should only welcome qualified like-minded competitors as A/Es on church-sponsored building projects in the developing world.

How Msaada Has Obtained Commissions

Msaada's initial clients included mostly Lutheran churches, missions, and related organizations, which I already knew from my time as a missionary architect in Nigeria and Tanzania. But we started out more ecumenically. For when Msaada Architects was formed, our first commission was for an already mentioned **Extension of Makiungu Roman Catholic Hospital** in Tanzania. Being asked to do that project was what gave the direct reason for Msaada Architects to become a reality! That was after I had met with the now late Sr. Margaret O'Conor, who was the administrative head of that Medical Missionaries of Mary Hospital. She later became a dear friend of my wife and I.

Note, therefore, the following excerpt from a 25th-anniversary letter, which Msaada received from Margaret: **"It was a hot, sultry day at Makiungu Hospital when I first met Poul Bertelsen. I had just left the administration building worrying about the condition of the Hospital. As I approached our house, I saw a bearded man in a short-based Land Rover pull to a stop. He waited for me and held out his hand [and said]: 'I am Poul Bertelsen'"**.

Sr. Margaret then added in that anniversary letter how she and I had been in contact earlier via mail, when she inquired if the national Lutheran Church in Tanzania (ELCT) A/E department might do a project for her. That department was so busy at that time that the answer, unfortunately, had been a "no." I therefore explained to her when we met that what half a year later would become the start of Msaada Architects was now being seriously considered. So, I inquired whether she, in that case, might still want me in such a new situation to work on the earlier required Makiungu Hospital expansion and renovation project. She quickly responded with: **"Yes, and God sent you."** She then added, **"Somehow, MSAADA was born there and then. I will never forget that."**

Do I need to add how I personally will never forget that situation, either?

That project was followed rather quickly by Msaada being asked to design a new, large **Bunda College of National Education** for The Mennonite Church of Tanzania through the Christian Council of Tanzania (CCT). This meant the new organization developed a good deal faster than had been expected.

The two projects in Makiungu and Bunda also meant our work was initially concentrated in Tanzania with a focus on providing A/E services on medical and educational projects, as had also been the case during the six years when the ELCT Building Department was transformed into an A/E Department. However, to avoid competing with that Department of the ELCT Central Office, we had not planned to do projects for the Lutheran church in Tanzania.

But we soon received requests to provide A/E services for a few ELCT projects. At first, I was reluctant for us to get involved with those projects, but we did do so after I had discussed them with Joel Ngeiyamu, my friend and former boss, when I had served the ELCT directly.

So, with his blessings, we started work on several Lutheran projects in Tanzania. Similarly, these grew to also include projects for the Lutheran Church of Christ in Nigeria (LCCN), the church I had served in Nigeria, as well as the other larger regional Lutheran church in that country, the Lutheran Church of Nigeria (LCN). The Lutheran World Federation (LWF) connected the LCN with Msaada Architects.

Usual Msaada Commissions

Msaada Architects' status as a registered nonprofit organization has shaped the kind of commissions we could accept. The State of Minnesota allows a maximum of 10% of the services provided by a nonprofit such as Msaada to be done for clients and organizations that are not nonprofits.

With close to 1,000 projects implemented by now — and with Msaada having worked on at least half again as many that didn't materialize — there are numerous projects to choose from to describe the organization's usual commissions.

The average size of projects Msaada has served on is close to 900 m^2 (or about 9,600 square feet) of floor area. There are also a good number of what, for us, are very large projects. But we have always preferred to have only one or two very large projects yearly as our "bread and butter" work, for we have prided ourselves on the fact that the size of a project is not as important as the value a completed project brings to the people it is to serve.

That said, numerous smaller projects would have been impossible for us to be involved with without the larger ones providing a steady income. Thus, to illustrate the diversity of our work, the following are some examples of what we consider medium-sized projects, with some bigger and some smaller than the average.

Msaada's involvement initially with a very large school project for the Arcot Lutheran Church in India, which will have its own chapter next in this book, led to us completing other projects for them as well as for other churches and organizations with Christian values in India.

Such projects include the **Renovation and extension of the Lebanon Home for Destitute Women in Tiruvannamalai**. The scope of this project encompassed renovating existing houses where the women live with their children, plus designing and building a new workshop where the women work on mainly weaving products to help cover the costs of their room and board at this valuable institution. The goods they produce are mainly sold in the U.S. and Europe.

The first request Msaada Architects received to work in Madagascar was from the National Lutheran Church's (FLM's) health organization, called SALFA. We were pleased to be able to design and see built, or expanded, a fairly large number of smaller hospitals and clinics for SALFA, which led to opportunities to complete medical and other projects for other church organizations in Madagascar, an example of which was the initial phase of a new **Baptist Hospital in Vaovao Mahafali, Mandritsara**.

We appreciated getting a letter at our 25th anniversary from that hospital stating the following after the founding missionary physician had explained his initial difficulties in getting a design for the planned new hospital: **"Thus, imagine our delight, on first coming to Antananarivo, to be told about a Christian architectural agency with expertise in medical buildings that had an office in the city!"**

The missionary physician went on to explain Msaada's thorough design phase, which involved a meeting in the U.K. when our resident architect in Madagascar was passing through there going to or from the U.S. on furlough. He added how Phase 1 was based on Msaada's design and construction drawings, while Phases 2 and 3 were also based on our initial concept designs as well as experiences gained from the initial building phase.

A Danish organization sending volunteers to many African locations prepares them for their assignments at a Training Centre in Arusha, Tanzania. Msaada has done a few projects at that Centre, including a **Meeting Hall for Volunteers**.

That Danish organization ended up also providing volunteers to serve in the ELCT. Three such volunteers were at various times in the A/E Department, with two more involved with other activities in the ELCT. The arrangement for the volunteers to serve for two years at a time was a result of me being asked by the Danish organization to teach the volunteers they were sending to different countries in Africa whenever there were larger groups of building professionals and/or craftsmen of various building trades.

Two additional noteworthy projects are the national **Roman Catholic Church Development Center in Lichinga, Mozambique,** and the preliminary planning and design of a **Roman Catholic University project in Juba, South Sudan**. A Jesuit Roman Catholic missionary priest from the U.S. contacted us about the university project after he had seen the completed Development Center in Lichinga.

Not-so-usual Commissions

In addition to working on projects from their beginning, Msaada Architects has also been brought in rather late in the planning and design stages of some projects to help revise designs done by other organizations, so they became appropriate and affordable to implement for the clients.

Such a project was **Housing for Surgical Residents at Soddo Christian Hospital in Ethiopia.** Another organization had provided designs with spaces that were larger than required and with structurally over-designed buildings. We revised those designs so there were sufficient funds to properly build the number of individual dwellings required.

Likewise, for a **100-bed Cholera Treatment Centre in Haiti,** Msaada was able to make radical changes to a design done by somebody else so the client could provide enough beds for cholera patients. The resulting facility was designed to be used later — when the cholera epidemic was over — to house the relatives of patients being treated at a planned future full-service hospital.

However, unfortunately, something went wrong, so the building did not end up with the quality of construction it should have had. For it developed some cracks due to the building site having areas with filling that were not properly settled. That was something which had not been considered, and Msaada Architects therefore learned a valuable lesson from that experience about how important it is to always consider even things that it might not have been easy to identify if not informed about it in advance by the client.

Before I was asked to teach at the University of Minnesota's School of Architecture, I was a guest lecturer there a few times. Thus, when a group of architectural students was given an assignment to design a **Model House for an Exemplar Village in Haiti,** Msaada's involvement was requested in the production of construction documents so the design could be built. It is included here, although it is a quite small project.

Further note that although that project did materialize, it was unfortunate how the "Exemplar Village," which was planned to provide rebuilding examples for houses in Haiti after the 2010 earthquake, ended up with many built designs not being culturally, functionally, or economically relevant for Haiti despite good intentions by the organizations that funded them. For unfortunately, many organizations seemingly lacked information about what was required in Haiti. This affirmed how important it is to include indigenous persons with any outside expats in the decision-making process for projects in the developing world.

Msaada was also asked to assist with another interesting project in Haiti, which was the rebuilding of a **Church and School in Petionville, Haiti,** which is in a very nice part of the capital city of Port-au-Prince. We were asked to collaborate with a European A/E organization that had already done some planning and design work. We completed the designs and provided on-site construction observation/supervision services.

Assisting Projects with Complications

As mentioned before, Msaada has quite often been asked to assist with projects in different parts of the world that had otherwise been handled by other A/E firms. We have been asked to do so in most cases after construction costs had escalated out of control due to a seemingly never-ending number of change orders. An example of which is **Tabor Church for the Mekane Yesus Church in Hawassa, Ethiopia**, which was a large new church structure for a very active large congregation.

Other examples of such projects include several with funding from the Lutheran Church Missouri Synod (LCMS) here in the U.S. and some in countries that were part of the former Soviet Union, including Russia itself. One such project was turning an existing multi-story building into a **Lutheran Seminary in downtown Riga**, Latvia. Additionally, Msaada was brought in to assist with projects that provided mostly new places of worship for national Lutheran churches, in Latvia as well in neighboring Lithuania.

While such work might not be the most desirable, there is true gratification in helping ensure that projects with problems related, in most cases, to excessive cost overruns will now still be completed, even if that might still happen with the original consultants completing the projects. Furthermore, a fringe benefit has usually been that, in most cases, such services have resulted in Msaada Architects later being asked to provide A/E services on new projects for the organizations we assisted. For the clients felt more confident that upcoming projects would be completed with quality construction based on appropriate designs and within the proposed budgets.

Thus, arrangements that were maybe more time-consuming than what we in Msaada were compensated for ended up benefitting the new clients while also presenting us with possibilities to serve on other projects later.

We have also assisted in getting projects done in Russia as well as in CIS countries that were formerly part of the Soviet Union. While such services were provided for the Lutheran Church Missouri Synod, we have served other U.S. or European mission organizations, too, mostly on projects in parts of the developing world on short-term assignments.

Other Partial Project Services
For the aforementioned projects that primarily needed assistance to be completed, it was not always agreed upon beforehand that Msaada's services should involve only one visit to a project, followed by a report suggesting how the project should move forward. There were also times when it was understood that Msaada should recommend whether the local consultants should continue to handle the project.

We have also had situations, however, where it was made clear to us beforehand that we would be making only one visit to a potential new project to help clarify what still might need to be done, including preparing a reliable cost estimate. We then usually assessed the situation, planned for remedial work, and provided suggestions for how the project could best be completed together with a reliable estimated cost — even though we would not be further involved.

This was essentially the case for a rather large **Lutheran Seminary Extension Project in Taiwan,** and Msaada was compensated for my time and expenses for traveling to Taiwan and preparing a report for a project which then materialized after consequent funding from the Lutheran Church Missouri Synod (LCMS) in the U.S.

After that, my only visit to Taiwan, I much appreciated a message from the local director of research and development at the seminary, which included this quote: **"I would like to present my heartfelt thanks to you for your interview and the written report to LCMS. Though your trip to Taiwan was quite intensive, you acted aggressively and listened patiently at all times."**

Later, for Msaada Architects' 25th Anniversary, an American missionary theologian's greeting included the following quote: **"MSAADA has been a real blessing to China Lutheran Seminary in Taiwan. Poul Bertelsen came to our seminary to evaluate our building program in January-February 2005. His time was filled with visits to architects, bishops, building committee members, pastors, professors, administrators, and many others. He completed a thorough study of the building plans, but his greatest gift was to listen and continually evaluate the project on a wide variety of levels while bringing them all together in a unified whole."**

These messages show how important it is to document the many aspects of a project like this in another part of the world for it to be funded. This should not only include information about a project's architectural design but also about how it will serve its purpose and function for the people who will use the new facilities.

Another example of such a project was a new **headquarters building in Nairobi, Kenya, for the Evangelical Lutheran Church in Kenya** (ELCK), which was to be built in the very center of this capital city. But while a local A/E firm had done an otherwise acceptable design the planned construction cost was too high for the donor to accept. Thus, Msaada was asked to step in and in a visit to the project location suggest how design might be somehow revised to be within a required maximum budgeted cost so the project could be implemented.

I personally have been on similar assignments in several countries in Europe as well as in Mexico, Jamaica, Columbia, Kyrgyzstan, Bangladesh, and South Africa. Not all have yielded the same positive results, and not all were done for the same U.S.-based national church.

A different example in Africa where Msaada provided such services was for a **Lutheran Seminary in Obot Idim, Nigeria.** We were helping to simply get a particularly complicated project underway, even though we could not continue to be involved because of geographical or other reasons.

After we had done that work, which also was for the World Mission Department of the national Lutheran Church Missouri Synod (LCMS) office here in the U.S., we received a letter from that Church's area director for that part of the world, which included the following comment: **"Not only was your advice sound, but you proposed ideas in a very appropriate way to our partner church leaders that helped bond us all into one team."**

So, although Msaada usually prefers to carry a project through from its outset to the full completion of construction work, there is a good deal of satisfaction in helping projects like the ones just mentioned to materialize. This is the case even if we are only involved for a short time, if other consultants take over the projects because they are located where there are other qualified A/E services available, or if there are reasons that make it inadvisable to have an outside A/E firm involved.

Another example of doing something rather unusual is when I visited the **National Lutheran Church in the Philippines** with the specific task of assessing all their properties to make suggestions about which buildings could be renovated or expanded, and which might be sold to obtain funds needed to complete the necessary facility improvements. I told the LCMS, as the Western client, how much of what I was asked to do could not be called architectural services, but they suggested I agree to do that, anyway. Msaada was again paid based on time spent and direct expenses, which in this case included making concept designs for the facilities' proposed expanded.

Many of the letters received from client organizations at Msaada's 25th anniversary stated appreciation for Msaada Architects being willing to undertake work that most architects don't typically do — or might even be unwilling to do. We believe, though, that whatever success Msaada Architects has had is a result of providing such services, and it is all best measured by what the people to be served by the facilities later have had to say about our work. We have thus been pleased to have received letters from numerous organizations or people representing the client partners for the local churches we'd served in the developing world, as well as from representatives of the client partners based in the Western world.

Turnkey Projects

It seems relevant to add here how Msaada, in the past, has quite often been asked to consider providing turnkey (design/build) services in the developing world. We have usually refused to do this so that we could primarily use our capabilities to serve on as many projects as possible. A few years ago, though, the Touch Foundation from New York City demanded that we use a design/build delivery process for some very needed expansion projects for **Sengerema and Shinyanga Hospitals in Tanzania** if that foundation was to provide the required funding for them.

We thus accepted and met that challenge, which meant we further did several other similar medical projects, mostly funded by that foundation in the same way. This all led to us again opening an area office in Tanzania for a few years instead of working solely with our local associate office. The involved projects, therefore, ended up being implemented, which, of course, was good. But it was, for us, later reinforced how Msaada Architects more economically can assist in the developing world by working as an A/E in cooperation with associate offices responsible for project implementation.

However, as indicated afterward by a communication from the one in charge of Touch Foundation's activities in Tanzania, the arrangement of doing turnkey projects required more of our time and presented additional challenges. Thus, we have not done something like that again. Still, the foundation's representative in Tanzania wrote: **"Although our common path has been from time to time 'bumpy,' thanks for all the hard work done for our foundation in the past five years. I am looking forward to other opportunities to work together in the future."**

Although doing turnkey-like projects in the developing world seems contrary to what I otherwise promote in this book — namely, for architects to serve more as true master builders — such projects can (in the future) also be within that particular function. This might be the case, for example, if doing so is decided upon primarily in situations where the project to be done is contingent upon Msaada agreeing to a turnkey format.

As I see it, the main drawback of the turnkey delivery process is that when — in addition to A/E services — literally everything on a building project is the responsibility of the master builder, there no longer is an impartial consultant who, on behalf of the client, can check everything done from the planning and design through construction, including the important monitoring of the project budget.

Bunda College of National Education in Tanzania

Renovation and extension of Lebanon Home for Destitute Women in Truvannamalai, India

Renovation of existing housing for women and their children

New Weaving Workshop

Baptist Hospital, Vaovao Mahafali, Mandritsara, Madagascar

Meeting Hall for Volunteers in Arusha, Tanzania

Roman Catholic Development Centre in Lichinga, Mozambique

Proposed Roman Catholic University project in Juba, South Sudan

Housing for Surgical Residents at Soddo Christian Hospital in Ethiopia

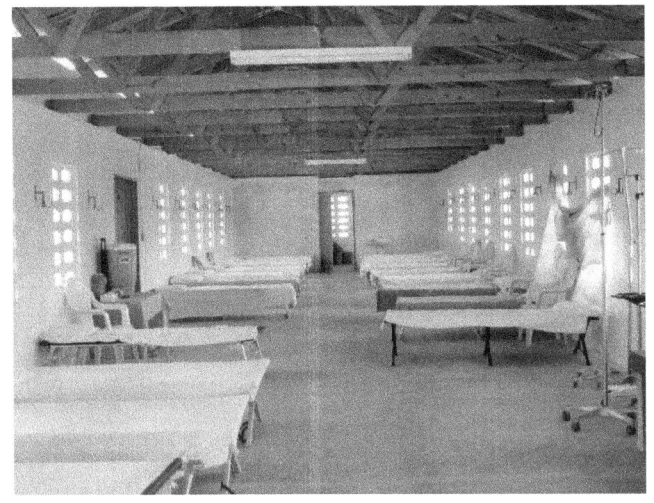

100-bed Cholera Treatment Centre in Haiti

Model House for an Exemplar Village in Hati

Church and School in Petionville, Haiti

**Tabor Church for the Mekane Yesus Church in Hawassa, Ethiopia
Showing structures to be replaced**

Lutheran Seminary
Expansion project in
Taiwan

CHAPTER 8

LARGE MASTER BUILDER SAMPLE PROJECT

The Arcot Lutheran Church School Project (ALCSP) in India was a very large project, or, more correctly, a series of projects that aptly illustrates the core values and skills that distinguish Msaada Architects as a Master Builder in the developing world. This chapter will address why that project was unique and, therefore, also became so important for our organization, for our clients, and not least for those many persons in South India who now use the ALCSP buildings every day.

Thus, tracing the history of how this project arose and the ways that it has so positively affected many of our global neighbors in Tamil Nadu, India, seems important. For that includes the many students presently enrolled — as well as those who have been enrolled earlier plus those who might be enrolled in the future — in the ALC elementary, middle, and high schools. Additionally, there are numerous residents who have attended — or will attend — adult education classes or benefitted from other community activities taking place in the new or renovated school buildings.

Introduction and Background of the Project
While the buildings Msaada Architects designed and implemented for the ALC School Project (ALCSP) can be looked upon as a single project

— as already mentioned --, Msaada dealt with it as a series of projects. The project holder was an indigenous regional Lutheran church in India with project funding coming from Denmark.

The project was initiated by a request from the Arcot Lutheran Church to the Danish Mission Society (DMS), which was later renamed Danmission, with the expectation that funding might come from the Danish government's aid organization, DANIDA. After that organization did provide the required funding, the DMS passed the intermediary responsibilities for managing the project and dealing with the Indian partner, the Arcot Lutheran Church, on to DanChurchAid.

DanChurchAid is not a mission organization as such. Instead, it is a church-related organization that deals extensively with development projects for churches in the developing world that partner with the national Lutheran "Folk Church" in Denmark. This project, therefore, also demonstrates how organizations with similar intentions for assisting in the developing world were willing to divide responsibilities based on what each of them was best equipped to do most efficiently.

Since DMS initially contacted DANIDA to inquire if it might consider funding a project to improve the physical facilities of the mostly dilapidated ALC schools, during a visit to Denmark by the first indigenous Bishop of the ALC I was asked to also come to Copenhagen to meet with that Bishop and with the DMS Mission Secretary for India.

By then, the DMS had already learned from DANIDA that an application for a project aiming to improve all ALC school facilities would be looked upon positively. A former DMS missionary theologian to India had, at that time become the Danish Ambassador in New Delhi. That was after he moved from being a missionary in India to becoming a Danish carrier diplomat. In that capacity, he stressed that "**all development likely begins with education.**" He had also become so attached to India that he easily moved from being a missionary in that country to being its Danish Ambassador, and he served in that position until he died in India, which had become his second home country.

When the DMS had completed preliminary investigations for the ALCSP, its staff realized they might not have the long-term capacity for managing such a project if, in fact, it would eventually encompass the entire ALC's school system, which had more than 90 schools. This is also why the handling of the project in Denmark for DANIDA was later transferred to DanChurchAid.

At first, I hesitated to get Msaada Architects involved with the project because we had no experience working in India. Further, Msaada was founded primarily to provide A/E services for church-sponsored projects in East Africa. By the time the ALCSP arose in the early to mid-1980s, we had already expanded our geographic focus to include other areas of Africa and the initial area office in Tanzania had been supplemented by area offices in Madagascar and later in Kenya, with the latter also serving as a regional Africa office.

However, during the meeting in Copenhagen with the ALC Bishop, the DMS Mission Secretary for India stressed his organization's reluctance to continue to negotiate with DANIDA unless I would commit to Msaada Architects being a part of the project. So, I agreed to go to India to do a feasibility study and a pilot project proposal. My decision naturally also was influenced by the fact that it was the DMS that had supported my wife and me earlier by sending us to Tanzania as missionaries.

The ALC Bishop stressed that he wanted the DMS and DANIDA to jointly help plan and design the project. I, therefore, represented the DMS as the architect in a two-person team chosen to prepare the feasibility study and pilot project proposal and I visited Arcot Lutheran Church together with a DANIDA educational sociologist, Lis Hansen, who had extensive experience in India.

Feasibility Study and Pilot Project Proposal
During the fortnight that Lis and I spent in the ALC area of Tamil Nadu, India, we visited a fairly large number of schools and met regularly with the ALC Bishop and other church officers. It quickly became clear that

there was a need for better school buildings as the existing ones were mostly very dilapidated. In some locations, teaching was even done under large shade trees.

To her credit, Lis rather quickly recommended that the project should also include an educational component instead of focusing only on building improvements. The importance of her suggestion became increasingly obvious during the two decades it took to implement the project because the scope of work included providing continuous education for teachers and ensuring that required books and other supplies were in the classrooms when the construction of each new or renovated facility was complete.

Later, adult education and other related programs were added and were to take place in the new or renovated school buildings. A health educational program was initiated also to ensure better preventive healthcare for students and for the general population in the areas where the schools were located.

Although the ALC initially was somewhat reluctant to include the educational component in the project, they eventually realized the great benefit of doing this. Once the building component was completed, the educational component continued to function for some years, with continuous education being provided for teachers and healthcare staff. The project staff was even asked to provide continuous education periodically for teachers in several government schools. This further increased the overall positive effect of the ALCSP in its project area.

After the building component of the ALCSP was completed, the ALC schools had a total student population of about 40,000, with individual schools serving from just under 100 to over 4,000 students. Three existing schools that had been renovated and expanded — two for girls and one for boys — had boarding facilities. Two additional boarding schools — one for girls and one for boys — were added in a mountainous area to serve a mostly tribal population. Two "Teachers Training Institutes" — one for male students, one for female students — were also added, as was an ALCSP Administrative Centre with offices and support spaces, a multi-purpose hall with an adjacent kitchen, and some staff quarters. That Centre's facilities were also used when teachers attended in-service training programs there.

One reason for the project's overall success was that it only included schools in the Dalit parts of the towns and villages where schools were located. The student bodies were mainly Hindus (about 90%), with smaller numbers of Muslim and Christian students. The schools are owned and run by the ALC as an indigenous regional Lutheran church, with teachers' salaries paid for by the government.

Building and Educational Components

While the ALC and the donors from Denmark viewed this multifaceted building and education program as one project, Msaada Architects, as already mentioned, considered it to be composed of close to 100 building projects because more than 90 schools needed to be newly designed and constructed, renovated and/or expanded. Existing buildings were renovated or expanded if they were in good enough condition for this to be a feasible, sustainable, and cost-efficient solution for many years to come.

While the initial visit for the feasibility study and pilot project proposal was my first trip to India, Lis Hansen had already been to this country many times. However, many of the interesting experiences that Lis and I had included how I initially was very overwhelmed when trying to communicate about the schools we'd visited during the first day because the schools' names were long, complicated, and difficult for me to remember.

Here, though, I will concentrate on how Lis and I developed a workable approach that demonstrated how and why DANIDA funds should be allocated for improving the ALC schools. Since we did not want to recommend that only new buildings be built, we came up with a rather modest pilot project proposal. That included a smaller number of schools, which also involved some with existing buildings that could be kept if they received various degrees of renovation and updating.

Lis and I, as well as the ALC and the involved organizations in Denmark, appreciated that the feasibility study was accepted by DANIDA for implementation, beginning with the proposed pilot project. During the initial visit with the ALC, I learned a lot about the cultural differences between India and other parts of the world. These experiences helped me better understand how to work and serve in India and, later, were also extremely useful when Msaada Architects began serving in additional Asian countries.

I also realized how much of the professional experience which Msaada and I had from Africa could be related to India also. Further, during my initial visit to that country, I had stopped in Delhi to meet with three female Indian architects who were serving on a health centre project in Tamil Nadu that was also funded by DANIDA. In Msaada Architects, we incorporated some of the ideas these indigenous architects viewed as important in India into designs for the ALCSP. Thus, I was surprised when I later saw some of the Health Centres that had been built as part of their project had not used the ideas those architects had shared with me.

I believe this showed how important it is to point out things that are different in a specific part of the developing world from what is common in the Western world. Fortunately, the Health Centre Project, which entailed building a rather large number of new such centres, served as an important comparison to the ALCSP, which was better implemented and ended up making it possible for that large project to eventually get a total of 10 phases and clusters of schools built.

This was partly because of the quality of work done in the design and construction phases of the ALCSP and partly because of what the ALC themselves did. In comparison, two organizations were set up for the Health Centre Project: one to plan, design, and implement the construction, and one to operate and maintain the completed facilities. That was different for the ALCSP, as the ALC Bishop, pastors, and other leaders were involved in the planning, design, and construction phase and remained in charge of building operations and maintenance once the facilities opened. Thus, they had a bigger stake in the results and a vested interest in ensuring that the designs worked well and that the project was implemented fully as intended.

That funding for the Health Centre Project and for the ALCSP both came from DANIDA illustrates why the Northern European governments have set aside rather large amounts of aid for projects done in cooperation between church organizations in those countries and their partner churches in the developing world rather than serving only government-to-government projects. Because church-sponsored projects usually results in better value for the money spent.

Since DANIDA's funds come from taxpayers' money, it doesn't fund buildings used for religious worship. Thus, none of the school buildings could have crosses on them or have spaces used primarily for religious worship. This is similar for projects funded by all church-related organizations in Northern Europe, which use government funds for assisting their partner churches in the developing world.

Phased Implementation and Staying Within Budgets
Getting all 90+ schools of the ALC rebuilt or renovated would not have happened without a phased approach to design and implementation, as well as accurate project cost estimating and management. When one building phase or cluster was completed, the next one would be approved for funding only if the previous one had stayed within budget. It was possible to achieve this requirement because Msaada Architects was given broad authority over restricting and issuing change orders during construction. On public interest projects, there are always many people who want to give input into the designs even when construction is underway. That can easily become quite expensive and result in significant cost overruns.

For the ALCSP, those wanting to do so included pastors and other church leaders, school administrators and principals, teachers, and, in some cases, parents also as stakeholders. However, while all these people were given ample opportunities to comment on designs before construction commenced for each school, during the construction phase, Msaada Architects had the authority to only approve change orders that could be kept within the available contingency for each phase or cluster.

That situation often created temporary conflicts because the ALCSP had so many stakeholders, and there was tremendous pressure to add things to the buildings during construction. When some of these additions seemed reasonable, it was hard for me personally to refuse what was proposed. However, it was necessary to do so to ensure that future phases or clusters would be funded, and thus also implemented.

To lighten my own work and involvement, I once suggested to Jesudiaan Inbaraaj how he, as Msaada's associate architect, might also get more involved in financial matters, for he and his Clerk of Works did an otherwise commendable job. But Inbaraaj immediately refused my proposal. To clarify this, he stressed how it was much easier for him to tell people with questions about financial matters that he did not have the authority to deal with such matters and then "blame" me for what could not be done.

Inbaraaj also suggested that as an Indian, it would be more difficult for him to be as tough as I needed to be when having to refuse what someone might justifiably want to change or add at a time when there were no funds left for that. For it was a quite clear demand from DANIDA that if one phase or cluster could not be completed within budget, there would consequently be no more funds available for other schools still needing to be renovated or rebuilt.

So, I had to accept Inbaraaj's suggestion, and I learned eventually that after the many temporary conflicts I personally had with local principals, teachers, and pastors, we would all rejoice together when another building phase or cluster of schools was successfully completed within budget.

Thus, it was also great for me personally and for Msaada to receive a letter from the then ALC Bishop John Franklin for Msaada's 25th Anniversary that stated: **"It is indeed a matter of great pride and joy for us in Arcot Lutheran Church that we have benefitted greatly from** the ALC School Project over the years — not only in terms of school buildings but also a good many facilities covering churches and related institutions in the ALC...all reflecting true Christian commitment coupled with a missionary zeal. For all these, I wholeheartedly thank Mr. Poul Bertelsen."

This nice letter was sent even though Bishop Franklin, and I had had some conflicts, including a serous one that arose during my initial visit to the ALC together with Lis Hansen. At that time, Franklin was one of two pastors accompanying Lis and me on our visit to various schools. That conflict could have prompted Lis and me to leave India, as she suggested we should seriously consider doing, even though that would likely have resulted in the project being "killed" before it had become a reality. Fortunately, things were settled with Franklin, and the ALCSP became a successful reality.

I might add how Franklin and I eventually became so close, that when there was a conflict later in a meeting that included a new project officer from DanChurchAid, Franklin pulled me aside and asked that I personally explain the situation to the DanChurchAid person, so things could be settled without further damage to the project. I did this, and we resolved the conflict so the project could proceed.

Special Design Challenges

Msaada Architects could not have provided A/E services for the ALCSP, which was such a large project, if we hadn't been able to use standard designs and standard details extensively. DANIDA would not pay fees higher than what local A/E firms would charge, even though construction costs at that time (and consequently fees also) were lower in India than in most African countries.

So, while some buildings had to be individually designed, such as the two Teacher's Training Institutes and ALCSP's Administrative Centre, Msaada used the same general designs for the 1,000+ built classrooms. For those classrooms, we developed two sizes in addition to labs and other special spaces for high schools. The projects for each school further included at least one of an identical **standard-designed teacher's quarter**, so, for practical reasons, there would always be a staff person residing on school sites.

Msaada further developed three different basic designs for school buildings, which were being used in:

1. **Rural areas**, where buildings were always to be single story with sloping roofs.

2. **Areas that were rural but becoming more urban,** where buildings were mostly single storied with flat roofs and with structural design done so, a second story can be added later if so required.

3. **Urban areas,** where buildings always needed to be two to four stories tall due to the very limited sites used for large, still-growing schools.

Unique Construction Challenges

Based on the mentioned design approach, Msaada Architects could prepare comprehensive construction documents that avoided the loose ends, which might allow the building contractors to later ask for numerous change orders. While the construction documents were prepared in Msaada Architects' home office/studio in Minnesota, daily A/E construction observation/supervision was handled extremely well by our India-based associate firm of J. Inbaraaj Consultants, and the two to three staff members Inbaraaj had most of the time assigned to serv as the clerk-of-works on sites where schools were being built, renovated and/or expanded.

Msaada carefully checked the work of the clerk-of-works architects/engineers (who observed and supervised construction activities) when I visited India for this project and to check on other projects about four times yearly. Inbaraaj and I also educated the staff members serving in this role about the A/E construction observation/supervision process, although it could be difficult to understand having to explain to them and to the building contractors and their workers again what to do if they were working on maybe their fifth school and already had received training from us during the earlier school projects they'd completed.

However, this is a reality often on projects in the developing world if architects want to ensure that high-quality construction services will be provided. Thankfully, while working on the ALCSP, there were numerous times when building contractors and their workers were extremely excited and grateful to have learned something new after they had successfully completed some work, although they initially might have objected to what they were expected to do.

Whenever I visited India for this project, there was a project committee meeting that included the ALC Bishop and other ALC officers. This was because they were naturally responsible for ensuring that the new school buildings were well built and, later, that the students received a high-quality education. The latter was managed by the Indian educationalist in charge and his staff.

In the same way I was checking on the building component periodically, there was a very experienced Danish educationalist (retired Teachers Training College professor) who visited the project a couple of times annually.

During the building committee meetings that I attended, additional suggestions about the designs were always made. I began to see a common theme. Someone would suggest construction details that helped ensure one desire or wish was met, but then usually overlook how something else would consequently be jeopardized.

A typical example was a wish to have windows and vent openings that allowed for sufficient cross ventilation in classrooms, which was necessary in the very hot periods of the year. However, the design also had to prevent any water from entering the classrooms during heavy South Indian monsoon rains. This situation was made more complicated by consideration of the overall construction budget and the need to have classrooms withstand not only heavy use but also, at times, direct abuse by the students.

Toilet facilities were also a common topic at such meetings, as a standard design with **toilets over septic tanks** was used. This design was initially developed when I lived and worked in Africa. It was so simple that I wondered then why I had not seen something like it earlier.

So, we thought such toilets would be a great improvement over the pit latrines used in ALC schools earlier. We, though, continued to have requests from headmasters and teachers for "Eastern" type flush toilets, but such requests were turned down as such toilets easily are plugged. A common way to "take care of this" in India is to use a metal stick to try to unplug them, which then easily destroys the "water trap," and a full toilet replacement is then required. So, using such toilets might have become an unnecessary continuing long-term maintenance expense for the ALC Schools.

Once, half a dozen journalists from Danish newspapers visited ALCSP locations together and wrongly concluded that some young women working on the construction sites were just girls who should be in school themselves. That resulted in a rather complicated situation as the journalists decided to publish their rather negative articles on the same day in Denmark. The General Secretary of DanChurchAid phoned me immediately in preparation for a press conference the next day.

So I was, fortunately, able to contact India quickly to get confirmation that the building contractors had not employed any underage young women to work on the building sites, which was what the journalists had suggested in their articles. Thus, I confirmed for DanChurchAid that what the journalists implied was wrong and suggested they should have concentrated on the positive aspects of the project instead, such as the ones pointed out at the beginning of a report done by DANIDA when the project was well underway, under the headline "**The Quiet Success of the Church.**" That report stated, among other things:

"The process, the special arrangement with the partners involved (DANIDA, DMS/DanChurchAid, and the ALC), and the result of the pilot project were evaluated by a DANIDA mission, and everything looked amazingly good. In fact, it was almost

'disheartening' to produce such a positive evaluation report. The original plan for the project had been followed, the time had been used as expected, and the quality of everything that could be measured was in good order."

After the unfortunate "scare" because of the Danish journalists' articles, it was nice for all stakeholders in the project to be reminded about such reports from DANIDA, the organization that provided the project funding. And a later DANIDA report concluded with the following statement after presenting information about both the educational and the building components:

"This time it was again almost 'scary' how much went according to what had been planned...or even better!... Therefore, maybe the situation is that there was nothing specific to point out? Instead, the whole project has been moving along in its own quiet and efficient way, with a lot of local involvement but also without a lot of 'drama.' Parallel with that, it carefully has followed the laid out plans and ideas for the objectives to be met...[this] is, in fact, the true story behind the project...and that is not a small accomplishment!"

A building maintenance program was also initiated to help ensure that the ALC took the best possible care of all new and renovated buildings after they were completed. Such a program makes a lot of sense in the developing world. Msaada Architects designed this maintenance program in close cooperation with our associated India office to ensure that it could continue to be monitored by them alone without further involvement by us.

Additionally, upon completion, all new ALC school buildings were equipped with a toolbox that teachers could use for doing required minor maintenance work themselves. A "jack-of-all-trades" was employed within the maintenance program to do larger, more complicated maintenance work.

In addition to getting a toolbox, teachers were also given instructions about how to address common, simple maintenance issues. A very applicable example used to illustrate the importance of maintenance was that when a hinge might fall off a door, that can be handled immediately by screwing the hinge back on again. But if that is not done, after some time, the entire door will be damaged and need to be fully replaced.

Reflections on the Project

Before closing this chapter, it seems relevant to include the following excerpt from an encouraging message received from Janne Garder at Msaada's 25th anniversary. She was, as a DMS missionary in India, the ALC's coordinator of the ALC School Project:

"I have enjoyed working with you, Poul, and with MSAADA for about 20 years. The service rendered for the ALC cannot be valued enough. But for MSAADA, there would have been no project. Many known and unknown friends who have been traveling in our area in India have been impressed by the many beautiful school buildings, hostels, hospital buildings, and churches that are the result of your work in ALC since 1983. Students, teachers, and parents in towns and villages are happy about their fine new school buildings and make good use of them. The great facilities provided by MSAADA have improved the standard very much in our ALC Schools, and we are proud of that."

And here is an excerpt from DanChurchAid's encouraging message to me personally at Msaada's 25th anniversary:

"DanChurchAid has been working with you for many years — in fact, since 1984! Without your expertise, your open mind to new architectural and construction challenges, your sense of mixing old, local building culture with new and improved styles and techniques, and not least, your special gift of talking to our partners in a participatory way, we would not have succeeded in carrying out our big projects for Arcot Lutheran Church and some other churches in India to everybody's satisfaction."

Finally, it seems natural to close this chapter with another quote, being one by myself which I used also in *Design & Dignity,* after I had used it earlier at times when I was asked to express about Msaada with reference to one project:

"I have often been asked: 'Can you explain what MSAADA Architects is about, using one project as an example?' The Arcot Lutheran Church School Project that provided 40,000 students with new facilities and adequate classroom supplies plus better-prepared teachers is the example I most often use! For what better way is there to demonstrate the value of providing life-enhancing services for our global neighbors than by smiling, happy children in over 1,000 new classrooms throughout the Arcot area in the Tamil Nadu state of India?"

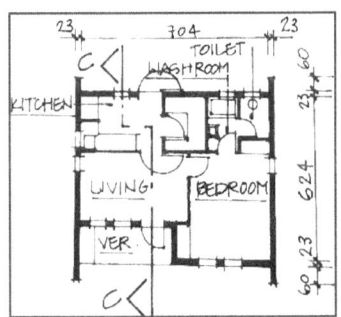

Standard Design of Teacher's Quarter at ALCSP in India

Typical Rural Classroom Building in ALCSP in India

Typical "rural becoming urban" building in ALCSP in India

Typical Urban Classroom Building in ALCSP in India

PART THREE

DESIGN
CONSIDERATIONS

CHAPTER 9

BASIC DESIGN CONSIDERATIONS

After now having shared how one large commission like the ALC School Project in India, which so aptly symbolizes what Msaada Architects stands for and how the organization worked and has served in the developing world for its initial four decades of operation, it seems right to share basic ideas and suggestions for how I personally - and thus also Msaada — has learned to handle designs on building projects for our global neighbors.

So, although there are some changes taking place in Msaada presently because of new leadership and because the organization is adjusting to the present-day situation of working and serving in the developing world - while being based in the U.S. — what is stated here related to the design of building projects continues to be extremely relevant and important.

Getting Involved with Projects in the Developing World

Another quote by the former President of Tanzania, the late Dr. Julius (Mwalimu) Nyerere, that I find inspirational and meaningful for serving in the developing world is: **"Human beings are indeed vulnerable when in need,"** and Mwalimu later proceeds to say: **"They can be destroyed as dignified human beings if required to submit to indignities in exchange for assistance from the Western world."**

Based on these powerful words, here is a list of important questions that Msaada Architects' design staff have traditionally been expected to address when starting work on a new project in the developing world to ensure that the concerns expressed so eloquently by Mwalimu Nyerere are always kept in mind.

- Who determines what will be done for the development and growth of church-sponsored building projects within countries of Africa, Asia, and other parts of the developing world?
- Who determines the patterns of involvement?
- Who defines the goals, priorities, and projects?
- Will the results be sustainable?

Msaada Architects' staff has, therefore, always been expected to ask themselves **"how much outside interference has been tolerable in the projects we have been blessed to serve on for so many years, and will the resulting projects be sustainable?"**

It is important to continue to understand why Msaada Architects was founded to serve in East Africa, initially, and later started serving in other parts of that continent, too, plus then also commenced serving on mostly the Indian subcontinent of Asia plus (on a more limited basis) in South America, Russia, several countries that had been part of the Soviet Union, and other locations around the world. The following principles have guided us throughout Msaada's history and, I trust, they will continue to be relevant for the design of building projects throughout the developing world:

- Msaada Architects has traditionally made all efforts to stay focused on how it was created as a response to specific humanitarian needs in the developing world
- Msaada Architects' purpose has further always been to primarily serve Christian churches, missions, and related organizations in that part of the world by providing appropriate A/E services for their building projects!

- Msaada Architects operates on a not-for-profit basis!

Important Design Considerations

A key challenge for working on projects in the developing world is the continued need to emphasize matters that are relevant for most projects in this realm, even though some of these may seem irrelevant to an outsider. This may be because the people living in the developing world during the colonial era became used to accepting that they should emulate what the colonial masters did instead of making up their own minds about what was best. Realizing this led Msaada Architects to create the following list of considerations, which I continue to see as essential for designing relevant building projects in the developing world:

- The developing world has valuable architectural heritages like Europe and North America. However, this fact is often ignored, in a manner like what occurred in the early years after the Colonial Era in the U.S., when European architecture was being copied extensively.
- Architectural heritage, especially in Africa, is essentially linked to life, where shelters from elements have been used for houses and meeting places for centuries. The "African Hut" has, therefore, always inspired me.
- Materials used historically in Africa include grass, banana leaves, skins, poles, mud bricks, rocks, etc. Thus, use those materials generously whenever possible, for they also result in buildings that likely will not disgrace the landscape as some new buildings at times can do.
- Recent building needs in the developing world have naturally also prompted the development of new materials and technologies. This has also led to more emulation of what is done in the Western world. However, that is often not the best solution.
- It is essential in the developing world to always be sure that architectural design is truly concerned with the real needs of

humanity. So, responsive architecture should work in in the favor of humanity by addressing the needs of the people who are to use a given building rather than being something abstract.

- Climate is a major factor in deciding the shape and layout of buildings in the developing world because it is usually not possible, for example, to have mechanical systems that control temperatures year round. Instead, designs must properly consider prevailing winds, average temperatures, rainfall, etc.

- Buildings in the developing world must be designed appropriately and with consideration for long life spans. Quick fixes often applied after a few years to new buildings in the Western world are usually not possible in the developing world, primarily for financial reasons.

Thus, when designing buildings in the developing world, here is a condensed list of things that I believe must always be considered:

- How can traditional shapes, details, and materials be used in new designs?

- Can existing designs be improved or translated into new technologies and materials?

- How can architects serving in new countries gain enough of an understanding of the local customs and culture to create designs that are as culturally relevant as possible?

- How can, for example, Western architects work in another culture or geographical setting and address challenges that are often related to their initial lack of knowledge about a place?

Finally, always check this list of absolutely required basic information related to project designs in the developing world:

- What is the climatic condition in the location of a project?

- How can designs for projects fit the natural habitat and environment?
- What is the required "human scale/human dimension"?
- Will the people later be "comfortable" in each space or building?

The 80% Rule

Experience has taught me that the final approximately 20% of a project's initial design process can easily involve as much time (and cost) as the first 80% of that work. This is because a lot of "fine-tuning" is often done to a building's design, which already might have reached a very usable and appropriate stage. Thus, for financial reasons related to working in the developing world, with partly Western staff, Msaada has historically completed most projects up to what I have usually called the 80% initial design stage rule. We have not achieved this ambitious goal though by sacrificing the quality of Msaada's design solutions but, instead, by making all efforts to reach an ultimate design solution as efficiently and as quickly as possible.

We have always done our best to ensure that this must be at least as good, or preferably better, than what others might often accomplish in the part of the world where Msaada Architects serves as A/E.

It can still be difficult to find experienced, professionally well-trained architects and engineers in many locations throughout the developing world. So, if a local firm takes over a project, the client might end up with a much less desirable design than Msaada Architects would provide based on our "80% rule."

There are, of course, some well-qualified and professional local A/E firms in the developing world, but they are typically located in the bigger cities and not in the rural areas where the need for better physical facilities to serve our global neighbors is most urgent.

CHAPTER 10

ACTUAL PLANNING AND DESIGN WORK

A fter having addressed the basic design considerations for projects in the developing world, this chapter will deal more with actual planning and design of specific projects as well as with meeting the expectations of clients. The latter is usually extra complicated because most building projects, which as an example Msaada has served on, have had, as mentioned often, a local client representative and one representing a financial donor from the Western world.

Initial Planning and Design Work

I've stated earlier how critical it is for the architect to have "two big ears and one small mouth" when commencing the initial planning and design of a project in the developing world. Over the years, Msaada Architects did develop techniques for making sure this "deep listening" occurs at the beginning of that process.

This includes how Msaada has realized that what — before the common use of CAD — was often referred to as "using the soft pencil" for sketches or concept designs should not begin **until after a preliminary space schedule has been done and discussed with the clients**. That schedule should show the different spaces or rooms required, as well as their proposed functions. After that, an initial cost estimate can rather easily be calculated based on the total expected project floor area if the level of a building's sophistication is also considered. For as it is essential that buildings in the developing world are structurally sound so they will have long life spans, it is fixtures and finishes that largely determine how costly a new building might end up being.

Such a space schedule and related cost estimates serve as a useful reference for the next conversation with a client, which should focus on what the client desires to accomplish with the funds expected to be available. Experience has shown Msaada that most projects in the developing world start out with a desire for a good deal more to be included in a project than can be afforded. So, it is important to equip clients with the information they need to seriously set priorities based on what is feasible to achieve within a set budget. There are now computer programs that make it very easy to adjust space schedules to reflect changing priorities.

It is a well-known fact, though, that the most relevant discussion about a new project in the developing world often takes place after an initial rough concept design is prepared. Because that **provides everybody with something to "react to" instead of basing comments on a more theoretical level about what is needed in new buildings or a renovation project**. This is also valid in situations where limited funds are available to alter existing buildings that are outdated for their present use but still are so well built and maintained that they can be improved and converted for new or different uses.

The emphasis on renovating existing buildings, instead of mostly building new ones, has been used extensively, for example, in Europe, for a long time. It needs to be added how that, of course, is easier when structures are made through extensive use of masonry and reinforced concrete instead of steel and wood, as is so common here in the U.S. But, when possible, it seems to have also become more acceptable to renovate in the U.S. as more building owners and investors realize that it is not always financially or otherwise feasible to build "new" instead of maintaining and renovating existing buildings.

Before coming to the U.S., I had never realized how the term "disposable buildings" can be used here, parallel with so many other things being "disposable" in this country. With reference to that, I heard somebody suggest recently, related to buildings as well as to other parts of what that person called "**the abandoned America**," how he sincerely hopes for a future where building on the past in this country becomes the thing to do instead of trying to somehow erase the past, as so often seems to be the preferred choice.

Thus, as a building design professional, I believe a new project involving existing buildings should begin with consideration for how these could be used for the same functions if they were properly updated and maintained — if that is what is needed. If this is not required, design professionals should consider how they could be remodeled for different uses.

Floor plans should be quite accurate during the initial planning and design phases of a project to devise appropriate concept designs with reliable construction cost estimates in the developing world. Further, it's extremely important to provide a bird's-eye view and/or a perspective drawing to support fundraising efforts versus generating numerous elevations and sections during the concept design phase.

Unfortunately, many projects in the developing world seem to have been initiated based on insufficient design and cost information, which presents challenges for all projects, but even more so for projects that are in the developing world, and which have a Western donor. Msaada Architects has learned the hard way that for the kind of projects that we have specialized in accomplishing in the developing world, even a small cost overrun on projects with outside funding will be judged more on when construction is completed than on whether the design is attractive and functional and whether high-quality construction has been achieved.

Thus, having initial concept designs with relevant, reliable cost estimates properly sets the stage for what follows. Msaada Architects' commitment to making cost estimates as accurate as possible has, as mentioned earlier, led to more than 95% of the projects we've completed to be implemented within their budgets. Accurately estimating costs from the onset of design and continually managing these throughout the construction phases of projects is an ongoing challenge because many local A/E firms and building contractors in the developing world will often start by suggesting low costs to win a project commission. Then, later, they expect to get change orders approved to make up for the difference between estimated and actual costs.

Once budgets have been prepared based on concept designs, it is essential to avoid the temptation to enlarge or otherwise significantly change the agreed-upon design as the additional design work proceeds. Also, there should always be at least 5% of an agreed-upon building construction contract available for contingencies when construction commences. Msaada has usually made it clear to clients that they should expect to have this 5% contingency — and, at times, maybe up to 10% — to cover changes that arise during construction based on suggestions from clients, building contractors and other stakeholders. Thus, when a project is implemented within budget, that means for Msaada, it was completed based on the original construction contract sum, with no more than the agreed-upon maximum contingency added.

During the conceptual design stage, Msaada Architects has found that adapting a design we've done for a client in a different country can help us to efficiently provide a good design solution for a new client elsewhere. Doing so enables us to quickly — and cost effectively — make a design available for fundraising purposes. So, Msaada has, for example, successfully used designs we initially created for building in one country as a basis for designing a facility with an identical or similar program in another country.

Observations from Early Msaada Designs
The back cover of *Design & Dignity* includes an apt, summarizing quote by my immediate successor in the role of Executive Director for Msaada Architects, W. Jerry Murray, about Msaada's design values

already from its initial inception. Jerry wrote that at the organization's 25-year jubilee as a kind of conclusion to what he had learned from working for Msaada as a young architectural graduate: **"MSAADA made me conscious that good designs can be derived as much from simplicity and function as from ornamentation and excess."**

The continued importance of Jerry's statement is illustrated by how he recently told me he believes that Msaada Architects' creativity and implementation of sustainable practices was expressed as well as it could be already in the staff houses designed and built as part of the organization's very first project, which was in Tanzania for an **Extension of Makiungu Roman Catholic Hospital**.

"Simple, practical but beautiful," is what Jerry said recently about those house designs, and he then added how they still represent for him **"the best of Msaada design"**:

1. Narrow building footprints encourage cross ventilation and simplify structure.
2. Wide overhangs provide solar shading.
3. Odor- and heat-producing rooms are separated from the living and sleeping quarters.
4. Outside yard space is utilized to give more usable space to the living unit.
5. The outside yard is further enclosed with a perforated wall, providing both air flow and security.
6. The simple use of a "Tyrolean" exterior finish (splash rendering or stucco) and the extension of the band with wing walls give simple beauty to the design.

So, Jerry concluded, "add rainwater storage and solar panels and you have the perfect sustainable house."

It is relevant to add how staff housing for Makiungu Hospital extension was based on a similar design, which was developed when I oversaw the Arch/Eng Department in the central office of The National Lutheran Church in Tanzania. That design was used initially for junior staff housing in the large project for the **Lutheran Junior Seminary in Morogoro** with duplex dwellings each having a courtyard for outside living and with living room and 2 bedrooms in a structure on one side of that open space, while the central building has for each of the 2 swelling units a kitchen plus toilet, shower and a storage room. This also meant sewage and mechanical systems for 2 dwellings were economically located there.

It was interesting through that while senior staff housing in that junior seminary project was upon request designed much like such staff housing in Europe and the U.S. we got when that staff housing had been occupied for sometime comments from several teachers asking why their housing had not been designed more as the junior staff housing.

Meeting Needs Different from Client's Initial Expectation
This subject was already dealt with generally in an earlier chapter. However, a simple example of giving the clients what they needed versus what they initially expected is the kitchen design Msaada Architects did for the **Kilimatinde Hospital expansion** in Tanzania. When we learned that a new kitchen was to be designed as part of a larger renovation and expansion of that Anglican Hospital, we wanted to talk to the head cook, as we would do with all essential staff.

At first, the missionary medical director objected to this. As expected, it was not possible to communicate verbally as well with the head cook as with other staff. However, a blackboard was available, and the cook was able to show with simple drawings what he wanted and needed. The result was a functional kitchen design that Msaada Architects has been able to use beneficially for other hospital projects in Africa. This would not have happened if we hadn't interviewed the head cook.

Msaada Architects' design for a new **Centre for Street Children in Nairobi, Kenya** provides one of many examples of how we gave a client what was needed and affordable by doing something extremely simple. We combined the requirements for a dining hall and an assembly space to create a multipurpose space. I have often been puzzled about why it can be so tough to convince clients that something as simple as a multipurpose space is ideal when there is insufficient funding to construct separate dining, assembly, and worship facilities.

In the developing world, Msaada Architects has further found that it is very difficult to get approval for a worship space to be shared with, for example, an assembly hall. We have learned that if this option is to be accepted by the local clients, we must at least include a curtain in the design so that the altar area can be hidden behind this when the space is being used as an assembly hall. This is because that area is the most sacred space for most Christian denominations. Many people in the developing world have explained to me, very convincingly, that the altar area must be kept separate and covered and, preferably, should not have anything that needs to be moved when the multipurpose space is being used for other functions.

A more challenging example of using spaces for more than one function arose when Msaada designed a new **Deaf/Blind Boarding School in Kenya**. The client wanted the classrooms and boarding facilities separated from each other. Because of budget restraints, we proposed and fortunately got approval from the client for designing spaces where students could both live and learn to reduce the total area requirements for the project because the budget would not have accommodated the original plan for having both teaching and boarding areas for the expected number of students.

Further, we addressed the students' double handicap by including plans to install extra-fragrant plants in outside enclosed yards to stimulate the students' sense of smell, thereby being reminded how important it is to let building designs relate to nature as much as possible, which was created originally with much more skill, knowledge, and wisdom than we humans will ever obtain.

It should be added how there of course also are situations where we architects have a wrong understanding of what is required or needed than does the client. An example of that was when Msaada had designed a new **Blind School in Antsirabe, Madagascar,** built for the National Lutheran Church in Madagascar on an extremely hilly site. For that project taught me how important it is for the architect to understand as much as possible how any designed facility is to function later. For when I visited the almost completed construction of that project on its beautiful site with existing trees and bushes remaining in place — primarily due to extra care by the building contractor — I felt we may have missed something which I now thought important.

I, therefore, suggested that maybe there should be more railings added along walkways to prevent the blind students from unnecessarily falling and hurting themselves. To my surprise, the indigenous female principal of the school replied by asking if I wanted to prevent the blind students from having the otherwise "normal experience" of all other children of accidentally falling and hurting themselves from time to time. I had certainly not thought of this! But that made a lot of sense to the headmistress of the school.

Working Backwards on Projects

Two rather recent designs for a **Lutheran Church/Community Centre and a Medical Clinic in Juba, South Sudan,** are examples of projects where the desires for what was hoped to be included in new buildings exceeded what could be done within the available funds. This was especially the case for the medical clinic, which was included rather late in the planning and design process. Thus, after a budget was set for each of the two projects, Msaada adjusted the designs so they could be implemented within the budget. Further, we allocated spaces on an already crowded site for future buildings that might be built later. The first of them was a now already completed expansion of the medical clinic.

Another recent example of realizing the need for a fixed budget and working backwards arose when Msaada was well into working on a project in **Cameroon** for an **Anglican Good Shepherd Academy** (Secondary School). This project began with much larger initial ideas, including by the U.S. donor, than what turned out to be affordable. Also, initial planning and design work had already been done by another U.S.-based architect as well as by a local architect in Cameroon. Thus, Msaada was asked to use that earlier design work as extensively as possible to save on additional A/E fees for the client.

We were already well into preparing construction documents when we realized we needed to work backwards to comply with a set budget while still meeting the minimal requirements for this facility during Phase I. The project was for a new boarding school that didn't have any existing facilities yet. Thus, as more funds would be made available, the plan was for more buildings to be added. Due to this approach and because of shortcomings in the earlier design material that Msaada Architects had received, four more buildings got added already while construction of the Phase I project was underway.

After that initial building phase was completed, we received this in a note from the Episcopal priest in charge of the U.S. board supporting the project. She also had initiated the project originally, together with the now late Sr. Jane Mankaa, as the local person in Cameroon: **"MSAADA's design of Good Shepherd Academy has set the standard for architectural design in the region. Sr. Jane is surely smiling on you from heaven."**

When Msaada was completing two projects in **Ethiopia** for **Aira Hospital and High School** funded by the Lutheran World Federation (LWF), a joint visit by a German physician and I resulted in new designs that could be built for much less than what the earlier designs would have required.

That physician and I recommended continuing to use local capacity as much as possible, which the local client appreciated. This meant the local architects and engineers used Msaada's conceptual designs as a basis for completing design development and construction documents and providing observation/supervision services during construction. The LWF accepted that, but I was later told the major mistake related to the two Aira projects was turning them back to the local architect.

That was, perhaps, only of secondary importance, as the high school and the hospital were built at a complicated political time in Ethiopia. I did learn from that, though, how, at times, one can maybe be too eager to promote capacity building in the developing world, even though I believe when we from the Western world serve there, we must always consider ways to help the local population develop self-reliance and/or build capacity.

Design Development

The conceptual (or schematic) design phase is usually followed by design development, which shows more detailed design aspects to be considered, including mechanical and electrical systems. However, the more that can be foreseen during the conceptual design, the more accurate the cost estimates provided to potential donors will probably be.

For especially larger projects, though, it is especially critical to have a solid design development stage before starting on construction documents, for it is our experience that projects reaching design development are likely going to be implemented. Further, at that time, the development of a facility's design should not only include architecture but also if — and to what extent — special structural, mechanical, and electrical engineering might need to be addressed also.

Construction Documents

Msaada Architects has never skimped when it comes to construction documents, which are called "working drawings" in most developing countries, for in my experience the only way to control a building process and the cost of projects in the developing world is to provide comprehensive construction documents, with everything shown or specified to the greatest extent feasible and possible.

This prevents building contractors from suggesting during construction that there are things they did not know about. However, a perfect set of construction documents has yet to be produced, and there is some satisfaction related to never reaching perfection, because you will continue to work toward that ideal. Thus, during construction, some funds in the contingency budget might also be needed to address shortcomings in the construction documents produced by us architects and engineers.

Since supplementing drawings and specifications with addendum (or change orders) is so common in the developing world, Msaada Architects has always tried to complete construction documents so well up front that addendum can be avoided or at least minimized. Further, instead of including "special specifications" to supplement drawings and *Msaada Architects' General Specifications*, we have always provided extensive notes on the drawings themselves. For while specification booklets often are missing on building sites in the developing world, drawings are seemingly always there!

Msaada Architects' General Specification is based on building standards set by the Royal Institute of British Architects. These standards have been used extensively in the former British colonies, are well known in those countries, and ensure acceptable quality of both materials and workmanship on projects, which is essential to always be aware of during construction in the developing world and in other places.

Msaada has also developed and used our own standard details and standard designs extensively for details or facilities that are reproduced in many locations, such as toilet buildings and water towers. This practice helps to make it economically feasible for A/E firms from the Western world to work in the developing world. Such standard details and standard designs seem the best and most economical solution for something that need not continually be reconsidered. While Msaada used standard details and standard drawings well before CAD was available, introducing that technology has made it so much easier to make those available for projects as might be required.

Staff Housing for Extension of Makiungu Roman Catholic Hospital in Tanzania

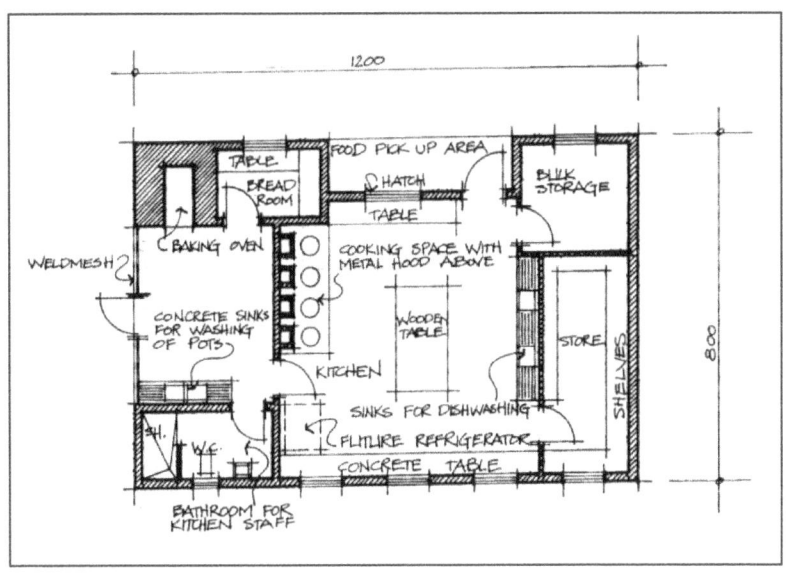

Kitchen for Kilimatinde Hospital Expansion in Tanzania

Centre for Street Children in Nairobi, Kenya

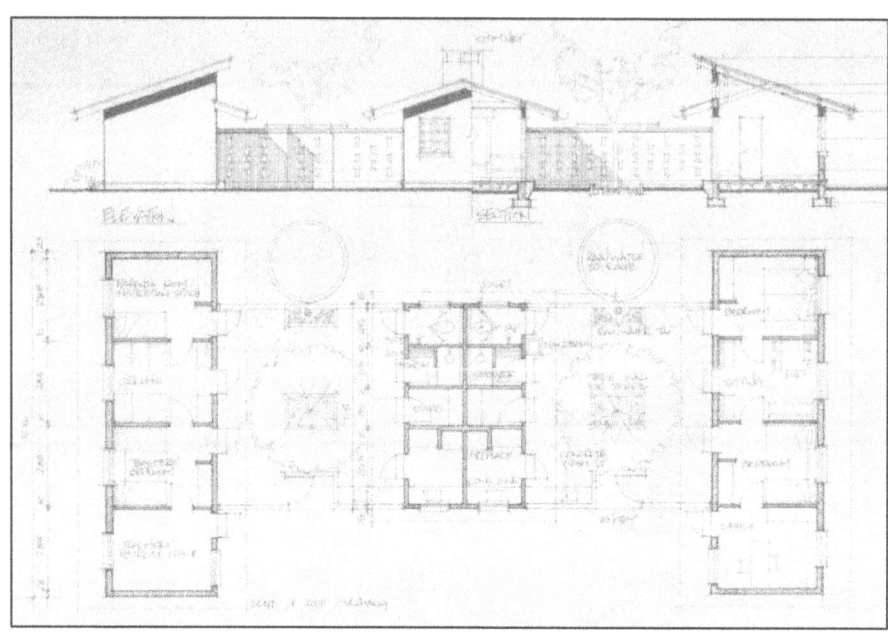

One of the units for the Deaf/Blind Boarding School in Kenya

Lutheran Blind School in Antsirabe, Madagascar

Lutheran Church/Community Centre and a Medical Clinic in Juba, South Sudan

Phase One of Anglican Good Shepherd Academy in Cameroon

CHAPTER 11

ADDITIONAL DESIGN CONSIDERATIONS

It seems natural that the two previous chapters be followed by one addressing specific considerations for designing of building projects in the developing world. These are considerations which building design professionals might not easily think about without a closer understanding of that part of the world.

Building Codes or Lack of Them

For years after most developing countries became independent, their building codes were based on those "left behind" by the colonial rulers. Although there are now building codes in most towns and cities in the developing world, this is not always the case in rural areas. So, as I have mentioned numerous times to co-workers, if there are no building codes for a project, we, the architects, and engineers, have an even larger responsibility to ensure that our designs are done correctly. For there is nobody else but us to blame if design shortcomings show up later!

Several expansions that Msaada Architects designed as A/E for **Tenwek Baptist Hospital in Kenya** fell into this category. This hospital has often been referred to as the largest mission hospital in Africa. It is in the central highlands of Kenya, rather far from the capital city of Nairobi. Thus, there were no building codes to follow when we designed those expansions. Still, the client was rather demanding, considering the level of relative sophistication of this hospital and the consequent design goals for new facilities of the American medical staff, plus the expectations of the missionary builders who usually represented the client during construction. So, it was essential that our Kenya area office staff were on top of what was expected and how they could meet the objectives for each expansion project.

I also recall a unique situation regarding the construction of a new **three-story office building** for the local Lutheran Diocese **in Arusha, Tanzania** because this illustrates the value of earning the confidence of local building authorities. In this case, there were both local building codes and building inspectors. The inspectors trusted the competency of our staff in the A/E Department in the National Lutheran Church's Central Office. They, therefore, allowed construction to continue while the city engineer was on vacation, even though that was when reinforced concrete footings for this three-story building were cast! This meant that when the city engineer returned, he would no longer be able to check those foundation's reinforcement because by then the backfilling had already been completed.

Long Building Life Spans with Reduced Future Maintenance

Since keeping buildings well-maintained in the developing world is a constant challenge, financially and because there is not as much of a tradition for doing this, it is important to ensure that new or renovated buildings will have long expected life spans and will not require maintenance too quickly or too extensively.

Thus, as mentioned earlier, buildings should always be built so they are structurally sound, while savings can be made on fixtures and finishes. In fact, if finishes are too "fancy", they will likely require more maintenance sooner. For example, it is more complicated and expensive to repair a floor with glazed tiles than one with a cement screed finish, which is, for good reason, still used extensively for floor finishes in the developing world.

It seems that while it is getting increasingly more complicated to obtain funds from the Western world for designing and constructing new buildings in the developing world, it is becoming almost impossible to secure financial assistance for maintaining buildings.

It was, therefore, also a very valid and meaningful experience for me when I was able to visit the earlier mentioned large **Lutheran Junior Seminary in Morogoro, Tanzania,** about 25 years after the initial buildings were constructed. What a joy it was to have my belief in focusing on structural soundness reinforced. The buildings were in such a good condition that a fresh coat of paint would have brought them back to almost looking new again after a quarter of a century of extremely heavy use.

However, while realizing that was great, it was even more valuable to be told how the Junior Seminary's Secondary School and Higher Secondary School sections had continued for a quarter of a century to provide some of the best academic results in Tanzanian secondary schools — and to be informed how many graduates had become pastors or, in other ways, leaders in the national Lutheran Church. Many others had even become people in various important roles or functions in the country.

The **ALC School Project** (ALCSP) also illustrates the value of structural soundness. After the initial pilot phase was complete, the donor agreed to the use of better-quality cement and better local building materials even though this increased construction costs by about 20%. DANIDA, as the funding agency, agreed that this was a good investment to ensure the buildings would have longer expected life spans as well as less future maintenance.

It was thus also valuable for Msaada Architects and for me personally to receive the following message from DanChurchAid's project officer after one of the early building phases of the ALCSP had been completed: **"It is indeed good news that the Phase III Building Program has now been completed. Therefore, it is important for me to stress that I see the completion of that as a very successful result and as a** milestone in DanChurchAid's and ALC's history. So, I want to take this opportunity to thank you for the highly professional job MSAADA has done and for your personal involvement and commitment to this project."

A restoration of an almost 300-year-old **Assembly Hall for a High School in Tranquebar, India** — which like mentioned earlier is a former Danish trading post in Tamil Nadu — provides a great example of how valid it is to make sure buildings are designed and constructed to achieve long lifespans in the developing world. If this building had not been done well when it was built originally about three centuries ago, it would not have been possible for us at Msaada Architects to ensure its restoration, even after the building had not been given any reasonable maintenance attention for a long time.

Choice of Building Materials

A new **Lutheran Church in Pangani, Tanzania**, which was completed when I was in charge of the A/E department in the Central Office of the National Lutheran Church in Tanzania, shows the pros and cons of using locally available materials. To save money and, importantly, to also create a culturally appropriate design, we suggested using readily available coral blocks for masonry work and banana leaves for roof coverings. In our view, this would achieve a beautiful new church that also related well to the site's location right next to an Indian Ocean beach.

However, the local congregation emphasized their understanding that the only types of buildings that used these materials were "tourist facilities and buildings constructed by people or groups who couldn't afford better materials." The congregation did not see themselves fitting into either of those categories. Thus, concrete blocks and corrugated iron roofing sheets were used, and I personally had another lesson about how a new building does not belong to the architect but rather to its future users.

While the developing world usually does not have the variety of building materials that are available in the Western world, Msaada

Architects has never considered that to be a problem. Instead, we have always made efforts to view this as a positive challenge! We have used the same approach to researching, recommending, and using materials across our projects, the large majority of which have had low budgets. Sometimes, though, other factors have affected such decisions.

As an example, while we were designing a new **Lutheran Deaf Boarding School at the East Coast in Madagascar,** Msaada was asked to use roofing material manufactured by a production unit established by a United Nations development program. We normally hesitate to use materials that have not been proven yet, but we had to accept and integrate that roofing material into the design of this facility as the client insisted on it.

A few years later, when a hurricane severely damaged or removed the roofs of the school while neighboring buildings with corrugated iron sheets had not been damaged much, Msaada Architects was now blamed for using the new roofing material. By then, the U.N. program had been closed, so there was nobody else for the client to blame but Msaada.

The picture from the school's boarding facilities shows a typical example in Africa of using bunk beds to reduce total floor area requirements for financial reasons. Something which is a step up from India where boarding areas like this still usually involve the students sleeping on mats on the floor.

A new **Lutheran Church in Santhapettai, India,** was designed and built as an anniversary gift to the Arcot Lutheran Church (ALC) in Tamil Nadu, India, from the Danish Mission Society. The budget for this project was not as tight as had been the case for other India projects Msaada Architects had been involved with, so we did not need to be as careful about the cost of building materials. However, we faced another challenge: The mission organization wanted what they suggested as an "Indian-inspired design." Initially, I also thought this was correct. But the ALC wanted what they called a "modern design," providing another reminder that a new church, as well as other new facilities, should be designed in accordance with what the future occupants prefer and will be comfortable with.

Earlier, I referred to an article in *Architecture Minnesota* (Nov/Dec 1989) titled "Mud and Mortar," which illustrates the variety of building materials Msaada Architects has used. That article also describes how we have found it relevant and appropriate to create designs for projects that can be built with quality construction that is based on good, functional design.

To summarize, we see it as a positive challenge to use local materials as much as possible on projects because importing materials from other countries means that a project will channel less money into the local economy. Further, the craftspeople in the developing world are more comfortable working with familiar local materials and technologies.

Avoid "Reinventing the Wheel,"

If a good design can be used in more than one place, Msaada Architects has never been bashful about doing this, as mentioned earlier! A prime example of that was when we were asked — simultaneously by different clients — to design **Outpatient Departments (OPDs) for two Lutheran hospitals** that had identical design programs. One of those hospitals was near Arusha in Tanzania, while the other was in Antsirabe, Madagascar. We thus used the same floor plan for both projects and only made changes in 3D due to different materials being available in each of the locations. Thus, the two buildings do not resemble each other as much as could have been the case, and they are further located in different countries.

By comparison, though, the OPD for the hospital in Tanzania had to be built with a steel structure because this material was donated to the project from the U.S. So, ironically, that project ended up costing more than the one in Madagascar, partly because Tanzania's building contractors and their craftsmen were not familiar with this material but also because for the hospital to receive the gift of a steel structure, the project funds had to pay for experts to travel from the U.S. to Tanzania to teach local builders how to use this technology. So, this is an example of how a well-intentioned donation from the Western world can end up adding cost to a project in the developing world.

New Jerusalem Church Project in Panruti, India, provides an example of how Msaada Architects was able to adapt a design we'd initially developed for a church expected to be built in Cameroon. The programmatic requirements for these two buildings were close to identical. Thus, we were in the midst of completing construction documents for the planned church in Cameroon when we had to stop work abruptly due to a completely unexpected lack of anticipated funds. Fortunately, by making rather minor corrections to what we'd already done for that design, we were able to produce, rather quickly, a full set of construction documents and reduce the fees to be charged for the church design now to be built in India instead.

In addition to using many building details again and again, through use of standard details, Msaada Architects also uses standard drawings, when appropriate and applicable, for services such as septic tanks and soakage pits and for small support buildings that have the same design program for various projects, such as toilet buildings for schools or even for medical facilities. If Msaada Architects had not developed a system for working on preliminary planning and design work for projects before funds were available in both Africa and India, the organization would never have been blessed to see as many projects constructed and used as has been the case.

The low cost of construction in the developing world, compared to construction costs in the Western world, continues to present a great challenge for Western architects working in developing countries. However, Msaada Architects has always seen it as being of great importance to make projects "happen," despite the challenges involved, for if a facility is never built, those affected the most are the people who would have occupied, used, and/or otherwise benefited from its completion, not usually the people who might have caused the delay or cancellation of a given project.

Appropriate Technology Considerations

It should be clear by now how important I believe it is to use appropriate materials and technologies for the design and construction of projects in the developing world. Further, construction should be planned so new buildings can be as maintenance-free as possible for years to come! In addition, Msaada Architects' objective of creating designs that utilize local skills and technologies helps to provide jobs for people living and working near a project site and to keep the costs down.

An example of this was when we designed a new **three-story Lutheran Centre in Moshi, Tanzania,** for a local Diocese. The client initially wanted a six-story building. But that would have required elevators, and these often do not work in the developing world. Msaada thus proposed and obtained approval for designing two three-story buildings joined by a common staircase instead. This eliminated the need for elevators and reduced the overall project cost. Also, the site was large enough for the expanded building footprint.

A couple of decades ago, Msaada Architects was asked to renovate parts of the original **Kilimanjaro Christian Medical Centre (KCMC)**, which is also located **in Moshi, Tanzania.** One of the new design tasks was to install ramps in courtyards. Since the elevators were often not working, the staff urgently required an alternative to stairs for transporting patients on gurneys between different floors in this three-to-four-story hospital complex. The KCMC had been built about the time Tanzania won its political independence and, thus; it was not sufficiently designed for its location.

KCMC has continued to ask Msaada Architects for A/E services while also wanting to support local A/E firms. One recent example of this arose when work on a new building that was designed as a Centre for Plastic Surgery was stopped when construction had only reached the walls being at lintel level. This was partly because of a lack of funds and, possibly, because there was not a high enough true need for this type of facility in Tanzania.

Msaada Architects was then asked to redesign the partly completed building so it could become **KCMC's Oncology Ward**, which would be the first such facility in a part of Northern Tanzania with a population of about 17 million. Although we'd been told by the U.S. client representatives that we could remove existing walls down to the level of the concrete floor slab, we were able to provide a design that kept most of the already built walls and added only a few new ones. This solution saved much in construction costs for a project with a very tight budget.

However, this also meant we had to remind the clients how a disadvantage of doing this was that the ward's design was not as ideal as it maybe could have been otherwise. Still, the priority for the local client was clearly to complete the project with the funds already available to provide much-needed oncology beds as quickly as possible.

In contrast, the U.S. client would have preferred to delay doing the project until more funds were available, and this thus became a rather typical conflict between the local client representatives, who needed additional spaces urgently, and the Western client representatives who suggested to delay until a more prefect design solution was possible. But the latter were not the ones working in the hospital and thus experiencing the urgent need for oncology beds, after some facilities for identifying cancer had already been built with funding coming from the U.S.

We appreciated though — after the project was completed and the new ward was taken into use — to receive a note including the following quote from the person in charge of the supporting foundation here in the U.S.: "**Working together to improve education and healthcare in Tanzania has been a real pleasure**."

Some **Baptist Missionary Houses in Nairobi, Kenya**, provide an example of a situation where appropriate technology had a different meaning than usually expected in that part of the world for us in Msaada

Architects. That was because those houses were built in one of the better neighborhoods of Nairobi, and for that reason, our designs included the use of materials that would fit properly in that location.

One of the buildings from the Tenwek Baptist Hospital, Kenya

Restored High School Assembly Hall, in Tranquebor, India

Lutheran Deaf Boarding School—East coast of Madagascar

Lutheran Church, Santhaipettai, India

Out-patient Department of Andranomadio Lutheran Hospital, in Antsirabe, Madagascar

New Jerusalem
Church in Panruti, India

Lutheran Church Centre in Moshi, Tanzania

KCMC's Oncology Ward

Baptist Missionary Housing in Nairobi, Kenya

CHAPTER 12

NOTE REGARDING CLIENTS

As mentioned maybe almost too often, most of Msaada's projects in the developing world have had two sets of clients: one representing the local church or another organization needing the facility when it is completed and the second being a donor from the Western world, which has provided all or a major part of project funding. This has often caused some complications, but we have always focused on seeing it as a positive challenge, as that made it possible for many needed projects in the Developing world to actually materialize.

But I will add also how, in my experience, the most successful projects are often those where at least a small portion (5% to 10%) comes from the local project owners even though most of the funding comes from outside. For some, local investment seems to provide a better sense of ownership for the people who will use a new facility, and thus, they often take better care of it, too. Here are now some of my reflections regarding how I believe it is best to work with clients on projects in the developing world.

Who to Work with From the Western World

If you want to meet the basic human needs of others as an architect in the developing world, it is essential to develop discernment. Applied to our profession when serving in that part of the world, this includes distinguishing between the projects you should undertake and those you should likely avoid. For example, Msaada Architects has been contacted by many especially Americans who were eager to become involved with the developing world at a time when they knew very little about what this involves.

This presents a great opportunity to teach and share knowledge. First, though, it is important to determine whether that person — or the organization he or she represents — is serious about what they want to do. What are their reasons for doing so? Do they have the means financially to do so? Without knowing this, it is easy to spend too much time on an endeavor that might not lead anywhere, as Msaada Architects has learned the hard way in too many situations.

The geographic location of the funding organization can be important, too. Based on the years when Msaada Architects served extensively on projects funded by the Lutheran World Federation (LWF), I learned how that global church body had realized that if it required funds from its member churches to plan and implement projects or programs in the developing world, then the U.S. is the right place to contact for emergency situations, which need quick and time-limited assistance. But if the need is for long-term, sustainable assistance involving erecting required physical facilities, it is usually best for them to contact the member churches in Europe.

As the LWF Department of Mission and Development is the one Msaada has been blessed to most often serve on projects, I appreciated receiving a letter from the Executive Director of that department, Dr. Christa Held, when she retired in the late 1990s, which, among other things stated: **"Since this is my last official letter to you, let me also here express my deep appreciation for an outstanding cooperation. It was marked by a clear understanding and easy agreement on all matters, confidence, and personal friendship. MSAADA has been a very valuable partner on large and difficult development projects, and we know (and admire) how much you personally are following up on all issues. May you continue to be successful, and God Bless you and your work."**

The earlier mentioned **Aira Hospital and High School projects** in Ethiopia are examples of projects where the Lutheran World Foundation (LWF) had me initially visit these two projects to determine how to reduce their scopes to fit within the funds available.

The LWF further asked that a German physician visit the project location at the same time, as he had been medical director when the earlier mentioned Kilimanjaro Christian Medical Centre in Moshi, Tanzania was being planned, designed, and built shortly after the independence in that country. The visit to Aira became a very meaningful and pleasant professional experience for the physician and me. For we were able to use our combined experiences to ensure that both the hospital and the high school project could now be built for the Evangelical Mekane Yesus Church in Ethiopia.

As too large projects had been proposed by the local church and their local architect, it was rewarding to create concept designs for both the new hospital and the new school that had the same basic capacities and still preserved some of the original design ideas developed by the local architect. So, the high school would have the same number of classrooms, and the same student capacity as had been planned for earlier, while the expected inpatient and outpatient loads for the hospital were also kept in the revised design.

The trip to Aira for those projects further involved a unique request to me personally. The local indigenous Bishop asked me to accompany him and some of his staff on a visit to the local governor so I could inform him and his Marxist government that while the LWF was ready to support development projects by that church, to serve not only its own members but the whole population, the church's main function is of a spiritual nature. Thus, the government should not, as it often did at that time, demand that congregations be closed in Ethiopia.

The bishop had already told me that, as expected, the governor likely would answer more agreeably to me. They would later remind him about what he had said in response to me when another congregation might be demanded to close. I was again reminded how extensively architects might need to be ready to deal with situations in the developing world that are unusual and can be culturally challenging. But I also admired the bishop for doing what he did, as that could result in different consequences for him than for me because I would be leaving Ethiopia a couple of days later. That also related to the fact that I knew the bishop's wife at that time was imprisoned simply for living out Christian values.

How to Best Serve Local Church Clients

As mentioned earlier, it has been Msaada's practice to be ready to serve local churches that require a proper concept design and related reliable cost estimates to use for seeking funding. We have more often than not done so with the risk of us being paid for those services only if or when such projects obtained funding. That required serious evaluations of such projects before those services were provided. But it is something that has been mutually beneficial for our church clients and for Msaada as well.

Such initial evaluations involve how feasible and needed projects are and how realistic it might be for them to obtain the required funding. That relates also to what our experiences have taught us about projects appealing to Western donors. When Msaada has offered such services based on us only being paid for those services, if a project was eventually funded, we have most often expected that when a project was indeed funded, we would continue as the project's A/E. For it has also been a lesson from the developing world that it usually is easier to make ends meet financially on later project work.

Clients Agree on What They Desire

Two new **Roman Catholic churches in Monduli Juu and in Monduli Town in Tanzania** are examples where both the local client and the donor representative had clear ideas of what they wanted and how these ideas overlapped on those projects. While the Tanzanians wanted a round building for the first project in an area of Tanzania dominated by the Maasai population, an American missionary priest at the larger parish was instrumental in providing the funding from the U.S. for both projects.

For the larger church, which is expected to eventually become the cathedral for a new Maasai diocese, the missionary priest had many ideas about how the architecture should support worship liturgies. It was thus meaningful after that church's construction was completed to receive a message from him, which included the following comments: **"The completed church is a strikingly beautiful building. When fully finished and used properly, it will be a wonderful ecclesial and communal tool into the next millennium."**

The now-late Fr. Gerry Kohler was that missionary priest. In 2005, he sent a letter to Msaada Architects for our 25th anniversary, and here is an excerpt from that letter: **"In the mid-1980s to early 1990s, Msaada was invaluable to me in two major construction projects."** Those were the two projects mentioned above, and Gerry later stated: **"I cannot say enough good things about the Arusha staff over the years, both expatriate and local, always with the backup presence of the home office....... May the good Lord continue to bless you with vision and good results for many years to come."**

Another project where both sets of clients knew what they wanted was a large project for expansion of the earlier mentioned **Sevamandir Girl's Boarding School**, an institution **in South India** where about 2,000 girls and young women attend classes at all levels, from elementary, middle, and high school through a Teacher's Training Institute. This series of projects arose and was implemented in phases because the head of the boarding school and the mission organization in Denmark that supported the school, were used to collaborating before the Danish mission had received funding from DANIDA, the earlier mentioned Danish government aid organization for projects in the developing world.

It was therefore affirming when the projects were completed to read the following in that mission organization's magazine: **"We owe a big** thank you to architect **Poul Bertelsen** and to his coworkers in MSAADA for the planning, design, and implementation of the DANIDA-funded project for Sevamandir. It would have been extremely difficult for us in Denmark to have controlled that project if we hadn't had an architect whom we could trust in all matters and who had both vision and practical sense in addition to an understanding of both the Danish and the Indian realities!"

Clients With Competing Expectations

A situation where the future user of a building and an outside donor had different expectations was **St. Timothy Lutheran Church in Bangui,** Central African Republic. Msaada Architects was asked to not only provide the planning and design but also provide an expatriate Clerk of Works who would, during construction, also function as kind of the building contractor with directly employed labor, as there at that time were not many qualified such building contractors in the capital city of that country.

This project developed into a horribly dramatic and extremely unfortunate situation as the initial expat Clerk of Works (Tim Olson) was brutally killed when he decided to vacation in a part of the country where foreigners were strongly advised against visiting. That resulted in me seriously considering that we maybe should stop providing the kind of services in Africa, which Msaada had by then specialized in. However, I was convinced that should not be the case. And consequently, much positive did happen because of this otherwise so unfortunate and so exceedingly sad event.

To begin with, the project was completed by another Clerk of Works from Minnesota (Tim Dray) serving on-site. More importantly, after the construction of the church was completed, the parents of Tim Olson took the initiative to start an organization called Lutheran Partners in Global Ministry. I had the pleasure of being on the founding board of this organization, which partners extensively with church congregations to provide quality education for people in the developing world.

Further, the church in Bangui ended up being very well built, and it was attractive, too, so the Africans were happy with this. However, a donor representative from the U.S. made it clear to me that he was not fully satisfied with the new church, which his congregation had contributed to financially. I learned this after that person, a pastor from North Dakota, had been in Bangui for the inauguration of the new church. Upon his arrival at the Minneapolis/St. Paul Airport, he phoned me and asked for a brief meeting before he returned to North Dakota. During that meeting, he told me that although the new church was nice and had been done within budget, it was "almost too nice." I understood this better when I later saw a perspective drawing of his church in North Dakota.

However, that situation gave me a welcome opportunity to explain to the pastor how construction cost is generally much lower in Africa than in the Western world, especially when using easily available local building materials instead of imported ones. I was also able to explain how labor is so much more affordable. In the developing world, building materials usually represent two-thirds of the total construction cost, while labor is about one-third. As is well known, the opposite proportions are usually applicable in the Western world.

This means it is less expensive to use local materials for design solutions that might be labor intensive. This is a skill and challenge when doing projects in the developing world for architects and engineers as well as for the building contractors and their crafts persons doing the construction work. But it is my experience that there are plenty of very qualified craftsmen in both Africa and India, and the money used for such a building project then has a larger, positive impact on the local population.

Related to the project in Bangui, it was very valuable to later learn how one of the construction workers for this project published a book in which he stated the following: **"We feel that neither the death of**

Timothy Gordon Olson nor the departure of his successor could squelch the harmony of our hearts, brought about through our close working together as we built the church. The story of the life of Tim is closely linked to that of the Evangelical Lutheran Church of the Central African Republic. He came to Africa for her, giving of himself to establish this church in Bangui."

Bunda Lutheran Hospital in Tanzania is an example of how difficult it can be to satisfy even one of the sets of client representatives if there are personnel changes during the project. A major design decision about where to locate intensive care patients in that hospital was initially agreed upon with the missionary physician who was expected to oversee this new 110-bed hospital after construction was completed.

However, that person was replaced during construction by an even more experienced missionary physician, who strongly conveyed that a different solution for the location of ICU patients was the right one. He also stressed that I should be able to understand this "if I knew anything at all about medical facilities in the developing world!" It was thus decided to follow his suggestion as his mission in Norway, which had arranged funding for the project, had told me before the meeting that we should make changes to the designs of the project based only on what I felt would be reasonable to do, as they foresaw that much would be challenged by the missionary physician who was now expected to be the medical director of the new hospital.

It was then later a strange situation when a third missionary physician ended up being the initial medical director for the new hospital. When I toured the completed facilities with that physician, one of the first things he pointed out was that intensive care patients would have been better cared for with small ICU's next to the nursing units in each of the four inpatient wards, as opposed to having the larger, central Intensive Care Unit that had now been built. Placing small ICUs near nursing units had indeed been Msaada Architects' original design idea.

The following excerpts are from a Norwegian newspaper article by the chair of the board of the Norwegian mission that raised funds in

Norway for the project largely through NORAD: **"When we today are able to see the completed Bunda Hospital, we know that it was made possible only because of the help of NORAD (the Norwegian Organization for Aid to Developing Countries), and due to the excellent cooperation with the Evangelical Lutheran Church in Tanzania. We also thank** MSAADA **Architects, who worked very closely with us in realizing this project. The new hospital is an impressive structure, which is in harmony with its surrounding terrain. The many different departments witness** MSAADA**'s careful planning and design work. Thus, the whole hospital complex presents itself as a very functional 110-bed facility."**

Later, the NORAD Director was quoted as saying: **"We got a lot of value for the money on this project!"** The hospital was originally planned to be built elsewhere in Northern Tanzania, but it was decided to instead locate it in Bunda based on a request from the Tanzanian government. It was, therefore, already, from the outset, a designated district hospital for the government, as had become so common in Tanzania.

There were also periodic conflicts between what the local clients wanted and the potential Roman Catholic donor organizations in the U.S. expected for the Roman Catholic projects Msaada Architects has done in Haiti. These created complicated situations for us, with the most challenging occurring in relation to the rebuilding of the large **Sacre Coeur Roman Catholic Church in Port-au-Prince.** We lost a good deal of fees on this project and eventually, we lost the project entirely during construction implementation because of serious internal disagreements between the various client representatives.

That is, therefore, a project where we may be justifiably could have chosen a legal avenue to set things right. But Msaada has never wanted to get into such a situation with fellow Christians, even on other projects where that might have been an even more obvious thing to do for other A/E firms.

Unavoidable Disappointments

After having shared appreciation from clients regarding Msaada's services as well as our gratitude for the many clients we have been blessed to serve, let me now include something about disappointments working in both directions. I am thinking mostly about the numerous projects for which Msaada has prepared initial planning and design services without us ever having been paid for those services, as the projects did not receive the funding that had been hoped for and expected. However, we have always accepted that this is what our system of serving was based on, and we've realized the risks involved were more than compensated for by the value of the numerous projects that have materialized.

So, while serving like that was part of what Msaada was ready to do, it is obvious that despite us always having been careful to only be involved with projects in the developing world which were truly needed by the involved clients and which we believed would be funded, there have naturally also been mutual disappointments related to those services.

However, without that system, Msaada would not have been blessed to see as many projects implemented as has been the case. Thus, the approximately 1,000 projects Msaada has now seen completed must be seen together with the large number of projects that were never implemented after Msaada had provided the initial planning and design services without being paid. However, we — often with great difficulties — made that system work quite successfully for four decades.

It seems important to provide a few examples of projects that illustrate the mutual disappointments resulting from that system by both clients and Msaada. The first is an **Affordable Housing Village in Liberia** that would have met a definite need in that country. We thought this project would be attractive for Western donors because it was expected to be less costly than construction usually is in Liberia due to the design proposing the use of old shipping containers — which were plentiful in the country — as the main structural elements.

Many people have, over the years, asked me why Msaada has not been more involved with housing projects in the developing world. I have often wondered about this myself. For that reason, we had high hopes for a **Dorcas Widows Village project in Uganda** to materialize. But that did not happen either despite it being planned with 30 housing units for widows with children to be used only for transition periods until the widows secured better employment and had increased their chances of properly taking care of themselves and their children.

Another project that did not materialize despite it being planned for meeting the important needs of women — which is critical in the developing world — was a **Village makeover project in Kisamis**, **Kenya,** which had a Women's Center, a Cultural Center, a Dispensary and housing for battered women.

Finally, I want to share how a project recently, which I was perhaps most surprised about not being funded and implemented with Msaada's involvement, was another Kenyan project for an expansion and improvement of **Consolata Hospital Mathari in Nyeri**. This project was initiated by the local Roman Catholic Diocese, which later "killed" it — after Msaada had spent substantial time planning and designing for it to materialize. So, we had another rather costly but also very educational experience about how difficult it can be to truly evaluate if a project without the required funding yet might actually materialize.

Roman Catholic Churches in Monduli Juu & Monduli Town

Sevamandir Girls Boarding School in India

**St. Timothy Lutheran Church in
Bangui, Central African Republic**

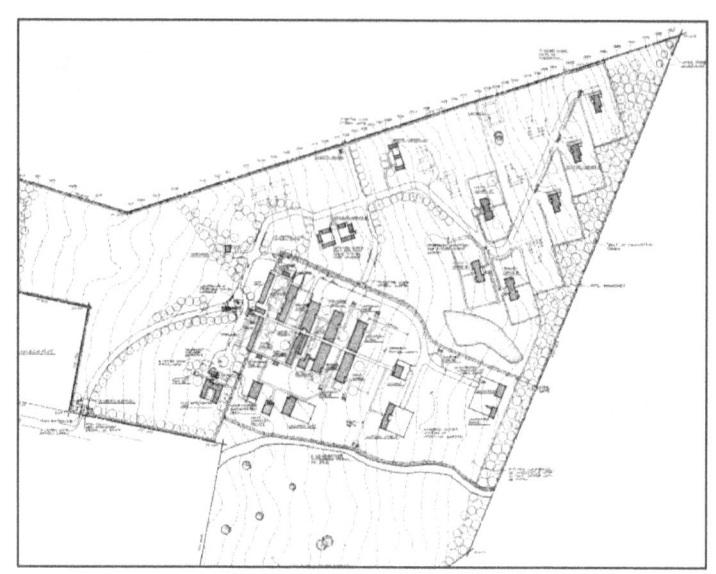

Bunda Lutheran Hospital, Tanzania

Sacre Coeur Roman Catholic Church in Port au-Prince , Haiti

Proposed Affordable Housing Village in Liberia

Proposed Dorcas Widow's Village Project in Uganda

Proposed Village makeover project in Kisamis, Kenya

Proposed expansion of Consolata Hospital Mathari in Nyeri, Kenya

CHAPTER 13

THE SIX S'S

To further emphasize what has been covered so far in this book, with the latest referring to design matters and project clients, it might be helpful to add more references to sample projects, as that is, after all, what design is about. I will, therefore, do so now through using the helpful prism of the "Six S's": **site, space plan, structure, skin, services, and stuff**.

1. Site

Msaada Architects has always taken extra care to create site plans that minimize the need to cut down trees, for in the developing world, trees are extremely valuable for providing shaded outside spaces. For example, prior to many of the earlier mentioned **ALC School Project's** new buildings in India having been constructed, the areas beneath shaded trees were often used as classrooms. We also changed some designs and site plans for that series of projects during their implementation, when doing so meant large trees could be saved.

Saron Boys Boarding School was one of the schools in that project in India. It involved an unexpected, different site design challenge. Because that school had a rather new toilet building, which really needed to be demolished if the site was to be properly developed. The difficult decision to tear that building down followed much discussion because of its financial implications. But it was clearly an example where a still-useful building on a site might, unfortunately, seriously have impacted future site development if it was not removed to give priority to overall better site planning.

So, although it was seriously considered not to demolish that still useful toilet building and replace it somewhere else, it would have been poor stewardship to have saved it. For demolishing it meant a large boarding school campus could be properly organized related to the different functions of teaching and boarding areas.

It was thus affirming later to see an article in a mission magazine by a now late Danish Bishop — who was the chair of the then Danish Mission Society — state: **"Saron has in recent years got some new buildings that have entirely changed the appearance of that old mission station. Earlier, it was mostly an old beautiful bungalow, maybe the most beautiful in the area, with some low school buildings and the church. But now everything has, through the additions of some large modern buildings, been joined together in a complex that is without its equal in beauty and harmony. It is a joy to see how new structures blend with old. And trees that were on site have been kept, and some existing rock formations have become part of an attractive rock garden."**

An example from Haiti shows how a desire to keep existing trees on site as much as possible can also create more challenges. When I, on project location, met American visitors from the organization behind a new earlier mentioned **Healing Hands for Haiti (HHH) Physical Rehab Centre in Port-au-Prince,** those visitors were so obsessed with saving trees that I had to explain to them the obvious fact that the required buildings could only be built if it was acceptable to remove some trees on a densely wooded site.

Isoraka Apartment building and **Andohalo Medical Centre,** both of which are in the greater **Antananarivo area in Madagascar**, and which were projects of the National Lutheran Church's medical department (SALFA), were both built on sites which the client had considered to not be usable for buildings due to their rather extreme grade differences. However, Msaada Architects' designs acknowledged the interesting sites as positive opportunities and not as problems.

Whenever possible, Msaada also tries to avoid what I call the "bull-dozer approach" to site development. This seems to be so common in the U.S., where sites are often leveled to fit buildings more easily. Instead, we try to have buildings grow "organically" out of their sites. An example of this is how we used a very sloping site for the rebuilt **Salvation Army School in Poirrier, Haiti.**

2. Space Plan

The sizing, sequencing, and configuration of building spaces and the relationship of interior and external spaces on a site can often be challenging. The **CASA Cyclone Shelters in Orissa,** India, that Msaada designed for Churches Ancillary of Social Actions (CASA) involved such interesting and challenging space planning for a project with 20 large and 20 smaller standard village cyclone shelters, which ended up being built on reinforced concrete "stilts." The buildings were to be large enough to house the entire village population, as this is required when the river delta where they are located floods. But the space planning also required us to consider other uses for these shelters when they are not needed for that purpose, so they are all now being used as elementary schools when there is no flooding.

One of the 90+ schools included in the **ALC School Project** was built on a "postage-stamp-sized" lot with the roof atop this three-story urban school building developed to be the outdoor space for the students to use during recess. Another school had boarding facilities on a very constrained site. Thus, Msaada put additional boarding facilities on reinforced concrete stilts next to part of the schoolyard that was not to be used for buildings. In this way, we created a roof-covered section of an open yard that could also be used for student assemblies.

A **Baptist Guest House in Nairobi, Kenya**, is one of several church-related guest house projects where Msaada had rather limited space on the site to work with. We created a central courtyard with trees and plants so guests can sit on balconies or covered walkways outside, which is pleasant year-round in Nairobi.

It was a different and more challenging situation when a project for Healing Haiti (H.H.) was to be designed and built upon a garbage landfill that stretched into the ocean. That project was for **Hope Church and School in Citi Soleil**, which is a high-crime section of the Haitian capital city, Port-au-Prince. So, the local staff in our Haiti office were reluctant to go there, and thus Andrew Ripp, as our expat resident architect in charge of that office, mostly dealt with that project himself.

Most of the landfills that led into the ocean consisted of plastic and similar waste material, which made it essential for buildings to be constructed on concrete piles rammed into the ocean floor. This made the project considerably more expensive than it otherwise would have been. It was further a design challenge that the lower school grades were to use classrooms located around a roofed area that was also to be used for church services on Sundays, but which was otherwise primarily a play area for the younger children. It was good, though, to see this unique project materialize despite its many challenges.

3. Structure

When the construction documents were nearly completed for a large new, 2,500-seat **Baptist Church in the Kibera section of Nairobi, Kenya,** Msaada Architects' then-architect/structural engineer "demanded" to have four reinforced concrete columns added to carry the center part of its roof. This is a common requirement for such a large space, even though it limits full visibility of the altar and pulpit areas for some people seated in an assembly. However, in this case, one column was to be placed exactly where the pulpit in the worship space was to be located. We were thus able to develop an acceptable solution which integrated that column so that it started out as a gothic-style arch, which, in this way, elegantly framed the pulpit, which is so important for worship in a Baptist Church.

We were surprised when representatives of the Roman Catholic Bishops in the U.S. suggested the design for the earlier mentioned re-building of the **Sacre Coeur Church in Port-au-Prince, Haiti** after the 2010 earthquake should have "base isolation systems" for foundations even though these are usually only applicable for multi-story buildings in areas with seismic activity. Our structural consultant thoroughly in-vestigated the feasibility of this approach before it was fortunately dropped as it was not applicable and also was far too costly.

As also mentioned earlier, Msaada Architects faced a significant structural problem in the design phase of the project for **St. Francois de Sales University Hospital in Port-au-Prince, Haiti.** A five-story building that had been located on that site had totally collapsed in the January 2010 earthquake, killing all the approximately 75 people who were in the building at that time. So, we had to accept designing no higher than two-story buildings, as the emotional scars after the earth-quake were still very "raw" for both the staff and the patients at the hospital.

Msaada Architects used a different but also interesting structural de-sign approach when the HHH Physical Rehabilitation Center in Port-au-Prince, Haiti, was to have an **HHH Prosthetics & Orthope-dic Workshop** added to it. To save on construction costs, we were able to use existing old shipping containers as the main structural elements for the workshop. Further, to save the most possible on construction costs, the containers were left as they were to a great degree and mostly just painted on the exterior.

4. Skin

An important part of the architectural design process for building pro-jects in the developing world is to assess when using local/indigenous materials makes sense. For example, Msaada Architects integrated the "Dhaji" method for construction into the design for the rebuilding of some **schools in Haiti for the Salvation Army**, for those schools are in very remote areas. Access to bringing building materials to sites was very difficult because the roads leading to these schools were in very bad condition.

The Dhaji building technique has been used since ancient times by cultures around the world. It involves creating a patchwork-style, timber-baton masonry system filled in with mud, stone, and other local materials that were easily available on or near construction sites.

Msaada Architects' designs for a new **Sambava Medical Facility and Bible School in Madagascar** for the National Lutheran Church used masonry walls at the bottom parts of structures to prevent termite infestation and then wood cladding from the windowsills on up. With the exception being that walls around toilets and other wet rooms were fully done in masonry. The structures used wood as a main building material, too, because the construction sites were located so remotely that cement and bricks had to be brought to the building sites by canoes.

The earlier mentioned **Ankaramalaza Lutheran Church** in Madagascar was unique when it was designed and built because of the way Msaada Architects devised to extend the capacity of this building three to four times a year when the congregation grows to several times its normal size for seasonal gatherings of the church's "Shepherd Program." Thus, the design featured a tent structure that uses the church tower as the "tent pole." Columns placed around the surface of the expanded space provided a system for securing the lower part of the "tent's roof."

I used that project as one of the teaching assignments I later devised for my teaching of architectural graduate students at the University of Minnesota because we at Msaada Architects thought that was a good solution for meeting an unusual space requirement. We later learned though that the local congregation eventually found financial means to expand the church permanently to meet the periodic need for a larger facility.

5. Services

Perhaps the most complicated issue related to services for buildings in the developing world is what kind of toilets are to be used by the general public. As mentioned already regarding the **ALC School Project** in India, Msaada Architects has experimented with various types of toilets, including a standard design, which we simply call **"toilets over septic tanks."** It is a design with a hole for each toilet space leading into a pipe extending down to just below the water level in the sealed center container of the septic tank below. Waste is contained there until it flows out through high-level exit pipes.

This system is a big improvement over a simple pit latrine. It is functional, not too expensive and hygienic if cleaned with plenty of water periodically. That is important also because the water level in the septic tank should always be kept high enough for the bottom of the pipes leading into the tank to always be submerged. Because if that is the case, the only parts exposed above from the top of the containment in the septic tank is the total area of the number of usually 4-inch diameter concreate pies, with one for each of the number of toilets above being emptied into the septic tank.

Otherwise, in the developing world, the challenge is often to decide whether to use Eastern-type toilets, which require users to squat on either side of a floor-level basin with a drain, or Western-type toilets. The first seems usually most fitting for projects in that part of the world, while the latter is often seen as a step towards further development by the local population and, therefore, is often desired initially by local client representatives.

Although Msaada Architects didn't have the specific expertise to design a project for clearing excessive amounts of surface water in a heavily built-up area in Port-au-Prince, Haiti, a Roman Catholic client for which we already had done other projects in Haiti asked us to also design and get built what was called the **Grand Ravine Project in Port-au-Prince**. As was the case for other similar situations, we located an experienced U.S. civil engineer who specialized in projects like that so we could design this project with the understanding that our Haiti area office staff would do the construction observation/supervision.

Msaada Architects also did a rather complicated **water-supply project for Sevamandir,** an earlier mentioned 2,000-student girls' boarding school in India. While, again, we were not experts in water engineering; we were asked to do this project to ensure it was implemented, as well as the building projects we'd completed. The project was thus accomplished after we had consulted with the same U.S. civil engineer involved with the ravine project in Haiti.

For most of Msaada Architects' projects, we must be aware of how much electric light will be required. While the capital investment for installing electrical services is not generally the main concern for the local client, the ongoing cost of electrical consumption is important. Thus, clients are often eager to install solar power generation systems to provide electricity and rooftop rainwater collection systems to meet the demand for water consumption.

However, these otherwise appropriate design suggestions are often dropped when the high up-front capital investment costs for them are realized. Very large water storage tanks are required if they are to provide water collected from roofs to be used for a good amount of time during the dry season in the tropics. And if solar energy is used to provide all the electricity required, large numbers of storage batteries are required. Thus, solar-generated electricity is often used only for critical situations, such as for night lights in a medical facility's wards.

6. Stuff

Although this heading in the "Six S's" often covers furnishings and finishes, I am using it to refer to some of the unusual experiences one might have serving as A/E on projects in parts of the world that don't fit under the preceding categories.

An example of a very unusual and peculiar situation involved a U.S. hospital's support for a very-much-needed expansion of the **Ngaoundere Protestant Hospital** in Cameroon ending up with the unfortunate result that funds already received for this expansion project were returned to the U.S. government based on unrealistic fears of what might happen related to that project.

The U.S. hospital's attorneys imagined there could be a negative impact on the services that the hospital was providing domestically because of its involvement with a project in Africa. Although these fears were unfounded and based on wrong assumptions, it was impossible to convince the U.S. hospital's attorneys to change their decision, even though much effort was made to do that, not only by us in Msaada, but even more so by the hospital's own surprised and very disappointed medical staff, who had been excited about assisting the hospital in Cameroon, which urgently needed the planned additional inpatient bed capacity.

A project for **Tartu Theological Academy (TAT) in Estonia** ended up being much more complicated than it should have been. Thus, it was not implemented at the time when Msaada served on it. A U.S. mission partner had provided false hope related to its participation in funding the project. Because of that situation, Msaada connected the project with a Danish Mission organization that was ready to consider assisting financially. However, this organization dropped its offer after it realized the U.S. Mission partner had no ability — or even a willingness — to financially support anything of the much-needed project.

That project, though, gave me a meaningful cultural and religious experience in another part of the world. This was when I, together with the Rector of TAT, attended a worship service in a congregation of Old Believers who had come to Estonia from Russia. Besides being Rector of TAT, he also served a Lutheran congregation and volunteered as pastor (periodically) for the Old Believers.

It was thus disappointing that we in Msaada were not able to see the TAT project materialize. Despite that, we received the following message from the Rector: **"Once again, I'd like to thank you for all that you've done for us, being a real blessing from God. May He bless** you, and let's pray that there will be something beautiful and fruitful from our common vision of TAT."

While Msaada appreciated having seen some projects materialize in both Latvia and Lithuania, we were also involved with a project in Latvia that similarly looked very promising initially, but ended up not materializing either. This was for a **Christian Academy in Jurmala,** which was for a Western project partner of the local church that had strongly encouraged the project but then failed themselves to assist it financially. Such situations are unfortunate and difficult to understand for our fellow Christians in other parts of the world.

For they in the developing world are mostly of the belief that all of us in the Western World are wealthy and we also are so, compared to the poor in that part of the world. Thus, like it for me has influenced what I now believe as being authentic Christianity, after having been involved with fellow Christians in the developing world for about half a century, I have also come to better understand why Christianity can maybe on the surface be more attractive to the poor, who mostly are like "hanging on a cliff" financially, than to those who after the colonial time have become the well to do upper class. A class which unfortunately not always is ready to support the poor in their own countries.

Saron Boys Boarding School in the ALC School Project in India

Classroom Buildings

Dormitories

Isoraka Apartment Bldg in Antananarivo, Madagascar

Andohalo Medical Centre in Antananarivo, Madagascar

Salvation Army School in Poirrier, Haiti

CASA Cyclone Shelter in Orissa, India

Baptist Guest House in Nairobi, Kenya

Hope Church and School in Citi Soleil, Haiti

Structural details from Baptist Church in Kibera Section Nairobi, Kenya

HHH Prosthetics and Orthopedic Workshop in Haiti

One of numerous Salvation Army Schools in Haiti using "Dhaji" construction

Details from "Dhaji" construction

Sambava Medical Facility in Madagascar

PART FOUR

DIFFERENT SERVICES AND EXPERIENCES

CHAPTER 14

BEYOND BRICKS AND MORTAR

As noted earlier, most of my work as an architect has been in the developing world working directly for local churches as a missionary architect or — for about four decades — providing A/E services as a cofounder and executive director of Msaada Architects.

So, it was only in the initial four plus years after my graduation in Denmark that I worked as most architects do in the Western world. That being the case is also because a different aspect of Msaada's experience serving on projects in the developing world has often included addressing more than "bricks and mortar" matters.

Being an Intermediary

Assisting local church clients in the developing world before actual planning and design work commences has traditionally included assessing whether potential worthwhile projects might be able to get at least part of their funding from the Western world.

However, after Msaada no longer served primarily on projects in the developing world with funding from Northern Europe, we often have had to spend much effort upfront — before doing the actual planning and design work — to help smaller U.S. organizations and individual U.S. church congregations determine what is most appropriate and needed in areas of the developing world where they would like to assist others.

Assisting in Securing Funding

Often, Western funding organizations have had an urgent need for a proposal with a preliminary design and related cost estimates. Thus, Msaada Architects has had several experiences where we had to respond to these organizations' "need for speed." But none became as important for us as the earlier mentioned **Bunda College of National Education** in Tanzania. That project came our way when I was in Tanzania for a couple of weeks, dealing partly with Msaada's early projects in that country, including the **Extension of Makiungu Roman Catholic Hospital,** which was the project giving the direct push for Msaada Architects to become a reality.

At that time, I was also in Tanzania to visit potential church clients. One was the Christian Council of Tanzania (CCT), and, to my surprise, they asked if I, within a fortnight, would be able to do a concept design with reliable cost estimates for Bunda College of National Education for the Tanzania Mennonite Church. This project ended up with about 8,000 mm2 (86,400 square feet) of floor space. Within that same period, I would also be expected to bring the project documentation with me to Germany so I could present it to the potential donor organization while I was passing through there on my way back to Minnesota.

As Msaada did not yet have an office in Tanzania, the CCT offered me a space where I could work in their offices, so I could produce the required documentation at a time when a German organization had suggested to the CCT to quickly provide a good project about that size. This was because the Germans had funding for that available before the end of their fiscal year, funds which would otherwise be lost, so to speak, if they were not committed to a needed project quickly.

I thankfully accomplished these tasks, and this brought Msaada a large, funded project ready for construction sooner than expected after the organization was founded. So, providing a concept design with reliable cost estimates very quickly was essential for the client, and it further resulted in Msaada earlier than expected becoming financially functional as a nonprofit A/E service organization.

Being the A/E on that large project, also led to the need to open Msaada Architects' first Africa area office, for it would have been impossible to provide the construction observation and supervision services for such a large project in Tanzania without having our own office in that country. W. Jerry Murray was the first person in charge of that office. At that time, he had worked part time for almost two years in Msaada's Minnesota office. After Jerry had agreed to go to Africa for initially only six months, he ended up working and serving there for about eight years. After being in Tanzania for a few years, he went to Kenya to set up an area/regional Msaada office in Nairobi.

Rather early in its history, Msaada Architects was as mentioned earlier also asked to provide A/E services for a series of new or expanded **medical facilities in Madagascar for the National Lutheran Church's Medical Department (SALFA).** This led to a sizeable part of that country's medical services being provided by SALFA. Among many positive aspects, because of that, those projects were so successful that the country's government asked SALFA to take over one of their existing medical facilities. Msaada getting involved with those projects was the basis for establishing an area office in Antananarivo. We also had an Msaada area office in Addis Ababa, Ethiopia, for a couple of years.

Related to the projects for medical facilities in Madagascar, there was a unique situation where Dr. Stan Quanbeck, a U.S. Lutheran missionary physician and the then head of SALFA, asked me to make an inquiry to DanChurchAid. He suggested that I Inquire whether half of the funding already obtained for an expansion of the **Antanimalandy Health Centre** in Majunga could be passed on to them as a "donation" if they then would attempt to get the second half of the needed funding from the EU, so they afterward could pass on the full funding to SALFA.

The DanChurchAid General Secretary agreed to do this after I admittedly had been a bit concerned about how to best present the suggestion to him. In fact, I likely only did so because Dr. Quanbeck asked me after Msaada had already successfully completed a good number of projects for SALFA. So, the EU did provide the matching funds, and another important medical facility was funded for expansion in Madagascar after involvement and assistance from three different continents.

When Dr. Quanbeck and I met initially, we spent a few days together in Antananarivo, the capital city of Madagascar, talking about the newly established SALFA and how Msaada could maybe assist with expected building projects. Almost 25 years after that meeting, when Dr. Quanbeck and his wife were retiring as missionaries in Madagascar, it was truly amazing for Stan and I to sit down and realize how much of what we had talked about a quarter of a century earlier had, with God's blessings, been accomplished.

Stan was knighted by the Malagasy government after his and his wife's many years of team service as a missionary physician and a missionary nurse in Madagascar and after the extensive services Msaada had provided to SALFA. Thus, we appreciated receiving a letter from Stan for Msaada's silver jubilee, which included this quote: **"The Malagasy Lutheran Church Health Department (SALFA) accomplished many building projects with MSAADA's invaluable assistance, which kept us from overstepping our budgetary restraints, kept us in line with standards of building construction, allowed us to negotiate realistically with contractors, and made possible the design of appropriate structures for the varied climates."**

A later publication by the Evangelical Lutheran Church in America (ELCA) indicated how, under Dr. Quanbeck's leadership, **"SALFA's medical mission grew to 50 Hospitals and different types of Health Centers scattered throughout Madagascar with about 100 Malagasy doctors."** Msaada is grateful to have served as A/E on renovations, expansions, or new buildings for SALFA.

Msaada also helped to bring a Lutheran church diocese in Tanzania, which desired to get an educational project, together with a U.S. organization. This led to the design and construction of the large **Peace House Secondary School in Arusha**. But serious conflicts arose between the donor and the local project holder. It is a recipe for disaster if a Western donor approaches a project in the developing world believing they can make all decisions because they provide the funding. That was the case here, and it is contrary to what I have experienced in the developing world, that everybody - rich or poor - has something to contribute to what is being done jointly.

Being a Catalyst for Funding
Msaada Architects has frequently been contacted by persons who believed we provide funding for projects in the developing world. That is NOT the case. But we have often been a catalyst by helping to find funding in the Western world for projects in Africa and India, in particular. This was also why, at the end of the 20th Century, it was so detrimental when European church-related funding agencies that had supported brick-and-mortar projects in the developing world switched to focus on funding programs. Many of those organizations had seen Msaada Architects' involvement in a brick-and-mortar project as a guarantee that it would be handled well and done within budget.

At that time, about 80% of the projects Msaada Architects had served on in the developing world were funded by church-related organizations in Northern Europe. Thus, in addition to doing some projects in the U.S. to make up for this loss of income, we also attempted to expand our role as a "catalyst" for funding projects by establishing the "Sharing the Blessings," the "Venture Development," and the "Seed Construction" programs. These three programs, plus information provided to local Minnesota Lutheran news media, became part of how Msaada promoted the Christian concept of tithing.

However, while those funding programs, as expected, provided several meaningful "project opportunities for interested financial partners," when Msaada got busier again, they were almost forgotten or, more correctly, not given sufficient attention. This is unfortunate, as they provided a great and meaningful way for donors in the Western world to meet needs in the developing world. We were, because of those programs, also able to provide our 501(c) 3 nonprofit status to secure funding for some other projects if potential funders did not have that registration themselves.

Antanimalandy Health Centre in Majunga, Madagascar

Administration and Classroom Buildings

Dormitory Units

Peace House Secondary School in Arusha, Tanzania

CHAPTER 15

UNIQUE EXPERIENCES

I have learned that what one might experience or be expected to deal with as an architect on projects in the developing world can be surprising. Thus, when many colleagues here in Minnesota have contacted me over the years expressing an interest in possibly working in the developing world, they have usually started out by talking about how exciting and meaningful such work might be. I can always easily confirm that.

However, when they then usually add how they believe I also must make good money from such work, I share how Msaada Architects' work is not as rewarding financially as working in the Western world. But I then usually add that while working in the developing world is exciting and extremely meaningful, both personally and professionally, there can also be many unexpected challenges that arise.

Unexpected Experiences
I have experienced many examples of how the developing world can expose architects to completely unforeseen challenges, such as when I first visited the site for a future **Gossner Lutheran College project in Ranchi, India.** I did so as a consultant for the Lutheran World Federation (LWF), as Msaada Architects had been asked to evaluate the actual need for such a project. However, only upon my arrival did I realize that members of a splinter group from the involved regional Lutheran

Church didn't want me there, as they believed the project should belong to them.

People from that group met me immediately upon my arrival at the hotel where I was to stay so they could give me a letter indicating that if I did not leave immediately, they "would not be responsible for the consequences!" Shortly thereafter, I met with the head of the involved regional Lutheran Church, and many from the splinter group demonstrated against us by holding up big bed sheets that had "Bertelsen go home" painted on them. Additionally, most of those in the rather large crowd were waving small flags that had black skulls shown on them.

That was quite a welcome to a location in India where I, at that time, had never been before! So, I was rather strongly affected by that, and maybe more so because there were no other foreigners, with whom I could share my concern. But as I afterward went to South India, I was then able to share that concern with the first indigenous bishop of Arcot Lutheran Church, whom I had come to know as a very wise person. With his encouragement, I ended up writing a positive report to the LWF, so a project was funded with a very encouraging result.

The college received funding for a project that met an urgent need for buildings to serve tribal people in central India at a time when the college did not have any facilities of its own — and when it already had a student population of approximately 4,000. The college had been using facilities at secondary schools and a seminary during the hours those facilities were not in use by their owners. These were not the most advantageous times for holding college classes.

So, it was very uplifting for Msaada Architects to get that large project done and for me to return later and note how the students and their instructors were elated to now have their own buildings. This affirmed my earlier decision to support the project. If I had not done so, the students and staff would have been inconvenienced, not the people who had demonstrated against me. And after the rather dramatic beginning for me with that project, a poem was read to me when I was leaving from that visit, which spoke about what I supposedly had already done to help make the project happen.

The following is an excerpt from a letter received later from the former female principal of Gossner Lutheran College for Msaada's 25th anniversary: **"The information about the Msaada anniversary filled my heart with joy and excitement. I felt proud that Msaada had completed 25 years of service to fulfill the three basic human needs: education, healthcare, and spiritual expression at the global level... Msaada has contributed so much throughout the world to fulfill the will of God and for the Glory of God."**

Another rather hard but also very touching experience happened when I went to India for a project that resulted in the construction of **Tsunami replacement housing in Southern India** in one village after the 2004 Tsunami had destroyed numerous homes in many coastal towns and villages. It was tough to meet with widows and children of those who had lost their husbands or fathers during the tsunami. One widow told me that the ocean, which she called their mother, had now turned against them. It was then pure joy to return later and visit some of the fatherless families, who were now living in the 71 newly built houses.

We also had the meaningful experience later of Msaada Architects — together with our associate India office — being the A/E on a new **Lutheran Community College in India,** for it was built in the same area with the specific objective to mainly serve members of families who had lost their breadwinners during the tsunami. The funding for that project had been raised by the Evangelical Lutheran Church in America (ELCA) in response to that natural disaster.

Other Notable Experiences
Among also unexpected but not as significant experiences, I have in India often slept in hotel beds in remote areas where the sheets obviously had been used several times already. In Tanzania, I once stayed for five days at a Mennonite Guest House where there was no water for

drinking or to use for washing or even for flushing of toilets. But with beer being available, I not only drank some of that, but I also had the highly unusual experience of brushing my teeth with beer. For, while beer was available, it seemed impossible for me to locate any soft drinks and not to mention drinking water.

It was also unique in a different way for me to visit Armenia in preparation for Msaada doing a proposed concept design to transform a former Soviet proctology hospital into a **Christian general hospital in Yerevan**. I was even staying at Echmiadzin, the Holy seat of the Armenian Church, in a guest house with a view of the Ararat Mountain, where Noah's Ark was supposedly stranded.

It was, though, rather discouraging to learn later that the project donor, a very wealthy American of Armenian descent, eventually did not want the design input we had provided based on my trip there, as she seemingly was a "know-it-all" person. And she did not want that although our design would have kept the existing multi-story building much as it was already, with us adding just a two-story building expansion at the entrance side of the hospital.

On a trip to Russia which also involved checking on a small **church project in Nizhny Novgorod,** it was quite a touching and unique experience when, at a small gathering, the city engineer informed me in a speech how he'd always believed that Americans were the enemy. So, with me being the "first American" he had met, he now felt different. I, of course, did not tell him that I am not really an American.

It was also an interesting experience in Kenya for Msaada to design a renovation of the **Old Main Building at Rift Valley Academy** because U.S. President Theodore Roosevelt had laid the cornerstone for this structure many years earlier. But unfortunately we only had a picture of that building before it was renovated to get back to appearing more like it did originally, as part of the renovation objectives.

As work progressed on the construction of a new **Lutheran church in Krishnagiri,** India, there were, at times, rather significant disagreements between the leadership of the local, regional church and the congregation in Seattle, Washington, which funded the project because their pastor was a former missionary to India. I learned more from that former missionary pastor about the importance of keeping faith, for although there might be challenges in the administration of the local Indian regional church bodies, the gospel is still being preached to full houses in congregations, and this will thankfully continue to be so also in the new church building in Krishnagiri.

When that project was successfully completed, due in large part to strong follow-up activities during construction by Msaada Architects' associate office in India, it was encouraging for us to receive the following message from the new pastor of the congregation in Seattle who had then replaced the former missionary pastor: **"The joy we all experience as a result of this new church in India, is due in no small part to your energies and professional talents. To God be the glory."**

Similarly, a project for a **Roman Catholic Retreat and Training Centre in Nairobi,** Kenya, was one where there were strong conflicts between the client AOSK (Association of Sisters of Kenya) and the funding organization, Porticus Stichting from Holland before Msaada Architects got involved as the A/E.

Thus, it was affirming during construction implementation to get the following message from the person, who at that time was resident architect in charge of our Kenya area office: **"We had an excellent meeting with Kristof of Porticus Stichting on Monday morning. To hear kudos coming from the same man who caused the sisters to literally cry on previous site visits was quite a commendation for both AOSK and MSAADA. The implications of this are significant, as the sisters largely give credit for the donor's satisfaction to MSAADA's assistance."**

I had a maybe also notable experience already before I was part of founding Msaada Architects. Because after I had returned from a bit more than a year in Nigeria as a missionary architect, Susanna and I were married in mid-1971, after we had been engaged while I was in Nigeria. Thus, after our honeymoon, I worked for three-quarters of a year as a site supervisor on a large construction site in Cincinnati, Ohio. A city where Susanna already had a good job as a nursing instructor, which she had only commenced working in from around the time I went to Nigeria.

I got the job as a site engineer at a time when it was hard for young architects to find jobs in the U.S. and I was hired largely because I had worked summers during my college years as a bricklayer apprentice, and further, because I had already done a good deal of architectural construction observation and supervision in Denmark.

"Fundi" Training Program

When I started serving the Lutheran Church in Tanzania with the assignment to develop an A/E Department in the central office of that national church body, our first project had a major problem, as it had already been funded by the Lutheran World Federation (LWF) to build a very large new multi-faceted institution. However, that funding was based on concept designs with related cost estimates that had proven to be insufficient or to be only about 2/3 of what was required. That was if the project was to be implemented as had been envisioned earlier, based on the funds already committed to the project by the LWF and by having existing large building contractors doing the construction work.

It was thus fortunate that the initial design for that new institution, which was the earlier mentioned **Lutheran Junior Seminary project in Morogoro,** was not that great, for that gave us the opportunity to plan for a combined approach to move the project forward, beginning with making the design more relevant to its beautiful site. That included having buildings be mostly one story and having them open up to outside enclosed yards in some of the staff housing and in student dormitories. This allowed for easy access to outside living, which is so important in warm climates.

This project also allowed me to use some of the experiences I had from my time working in Nigeria, which related not only to designing in a tropical African country but also to ensuring getting construction done for a reasonable cost.

So, after the Junior Seminary project was redesigned with the same program as earlier and a total floor area close to what was planned for before, we could try something new to save more on construction costs — something I had considered doing in Nigeria but could not do because projects there were done mostly with the church's own building department functioning as the general building contractor.

However, I now could propose my idea in Tanzania, which, of course, was rather risky, considering I was so new in that country. Fortunately, I had already observed how the indigenous General Secretary of the national Evangelical Lutheran Church in Tanzania was somebody open to "thinking outside the box."

I, therefore, suggested trying to reach the budgeted cost by locating some good "fundis" (craftsmen in Swahili) and turning them into small building contractors by developing a training program for them. That program included giving them contracts with just one or two smaller buildings each, to begin with, and giving them reasonable advance payments as part of these contracts, as they did not have the cash flow to get started without that.

Later, it was then extra exciting for me to sign for quite a number of those "fundis" becoming certified building contractors in Tanzania after they had worked on that large project. One which was to develop a full Secondary School (Ordinary level) plus a Higher Secondary School (Advanced level) as well as a Continuing Education Training Center for different types of church workers, which included a Swahili language Training Centre for missionaries coming from the Western world.

The project also included boarding facilities for all students on campus, plus a required large assembly hall, dining halls, and related kitchens. Additionally, there was a church for worship plus several staff housing units for both senior and junior support staff. This was all located on a beautiful 60-acre site with a view towards a mountain from where it proved possible to obtain a great water source. So, everything worked out well for that project despite its cost having been significantly underestimated initially.

Msaada Architects later considered starting something like that "fundi" training program for the construction of projects in Haiti. But that would not work there. So, instead, we got more set on using already established smaller local building contractors with low overhead costs and an interest in learning, as opposed to large building contractors with large overhead costs who required higher compensation.

Let me add how great builders can develop without much theoretical training. An example is a foreman for a building contractor, Daniel, who Msaada Architects has used on many complicated projects in India. He always does extremely well, although his formal education is only four years of elementary school. When we needed a building contractor on challenging projects, including the earlier mentioned restoration of the 300-year-old **Church of Zion in Tranquebar**, India, Daniel was who we requested to oversee work on-site for a building contractor, whom we used a lot because of their good work, as he could do things other foremen with engineering degrees often could not do.

I might add to that how Africa Msaada's area offices have in the past often used as Clerk of Works local persons who did not have architectural or engineering diplomas or degrees but who instead had worked like the foreman in India and learned extremely well from very valuable practical building experiences.

Gossner Lutheran College in Ranchi, India

Tsunami replacement Housing in India

Lutheran Community College in India

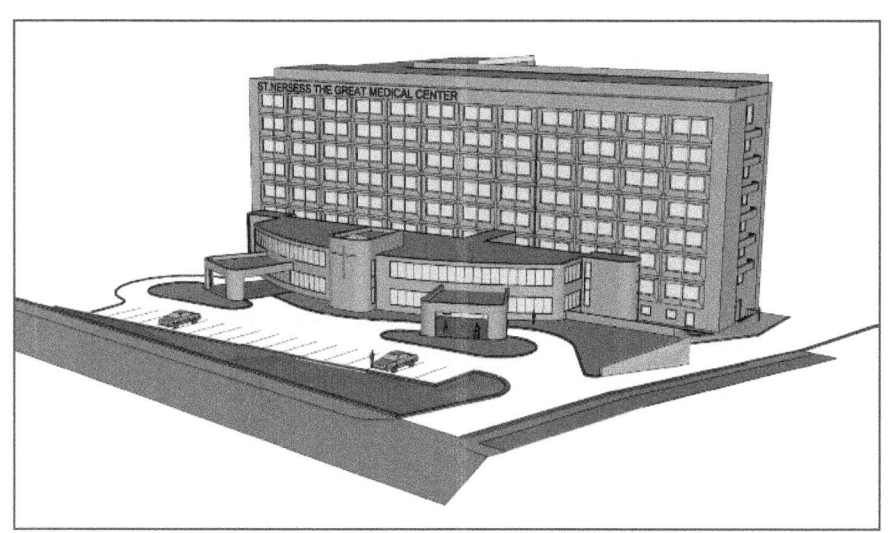

Christian General Hospital in Yerevan, Armenia

Old main building of Rift Valley Academy in Kenya

Lutheran Church in Krishnagiri, India

Roman Catholic Retreat and Training Centre in Nairobi, Kenya

CHAPTER 16

PROJECT IMPLEMENTATION CHALLENGES

I now want to share some challenges related to the work and services on projects in the developing world that might be required to get construction underway, as well as sharing some mostly unexpected experiences during the implementation of projects.

Dealing with Local Authorities
A usual challenge in the developing world is getting a project approved by the local authorities. For example, while working on the new **Lutheran Church Centre in the suburb of Jerusalem in Nairobi, Kenya,** during the six years I oversaw the A/E Department for the National Lutheran Church in Tanzania, I was getting tired of having to travel for about 4½ hours each way by car from Arusha, Tanzania to Nairobi, Kenya to continue answering questions by the city authorities — especially because these questions had been addressed by the project drawings and specifications or in subsequent communication.

Thus, the building contractor suggested that he instead apply for the building permit, and he then obtained that the next day! Of course, I had a good idea about how he did this. Thus, that situation taught me to distinguish between a "bribe" and a "tip," with me now having believed for a long time the latter is acceptable in the developing world. For that is tipping people who are paid a salary so low that they can't live on it for moving papers from one office to the next in a bureaucratic system. If that might feel better for some, it can also be called ransom paid for the release of documents. But whatever it is called, is it different from tipping servers in restaurants in the U.S. when their salary is too low to cover their living expenses?

In India, it is generally easy to get permission to build. The true challenge is to secure the "stability certificate" after construction is completed. Getting this official document, which confirms the structural soundness and safety of a building, is usually the responsibility of the building contractor.

Related generally to challenges due to corruption in many parts of the developing world, a Finance Minister of Uganda suggested to me how corruption on projects in the developing world could be reduced or prevented by making it easier for those involved in a project to resist temptation. When he and I, by chance, were seated next to each other on a flight in East Africa, he recommended that there should ideally always be a smaller amount of funds available for administrative work done by the project holder. This is something that I later promoted whenever I have been able to do so.

A relevant reference regarding what bribing might be related to a project for **Kagando Baptist Hospital in Uganda.** I was worried about going to Uganda for that project at a time when Idi Amin was president, and that country was in turmoil. But that trip ended up being a very uplifting and even a strong spiritual experience for me. Although, upon arriving in Uganda, I had one of the most unnerving experiences during my years working and living in Africa.

When a pilot of Indian descent, the British Baptist missionary physician in charge of Kagando Hospital, and I arrived at the small airport nearest to the hospital in a four-seater Mission Aviation Fellowship aircraft, some military personnel claimed we did not have the correct papers to enter Uganda. So, we were held at gunpoint, which was unnerving because the soldiers were rather drunk. While Rob, the British missionary physician, and I had been talking on the plane about how it can be dangerous to give in to bribing authorities in difficult situations, we were allowed to enter Uganda only after Rob provided the soldiers with medicine to treat gonorrhea.

Thus, after we had left the airport, I asked Rob whether he had treated patients with the medicine or whether he had bribed the soldiers. This was obviously a difficult question. But later, it was very rewarding to see how a hospital with buildings that initially were mainly mud and stick structures or metal storage huts without any windows ended up against all odds to be turned into a functional 120-bed hospital with well-designed and generally well-constructed buildings.

I further had the spiritual experience during that first visit to Kagando of worshipping with a joyful Baptist congregation that had — during the preceding week — lost a couple of members who had been taken into the mountains to be killed just for professing to be Christians. It was an uplifting experience based on an otherwise terribly sad development. So, after the not-so-pleasant welcome to Uganda, I could leave a few days later, giving thanks to God for the opportunity to serve there.

Over the years, it has been encouraging to have noted how African governments often look to churches to help meet the needs of their people. Thus, in Tanzania, many of the projects for hospital facilities that Msaada has seen completed are now functioning as "Designated District Hospitals" in locations where the government does not have such a facility itself. Additionally, the successful expansion of many of the national Lutheran Church's medical facilities in Madagascar and the improvement of existing facilities further meant that at least one existing government facility was passed on to the church to own and operate.

Material Procurement Program

When, for an extended period, there were shortages of building materials in Tanzania, Msaada began a "procurement program to obtain materials" for our A/E projects in that country. This entailed importing materials from neighboring countries, such as Kenya, and when so required, also from the Western world. To do this, we needed to be precise when measuring quantities to ensure there was enough material, but not too much, as that would increase project costs.

Measuring quantities for a project was, though, already a well-known practice in Tanzania, as completing "Bills of Quantities" by so-called "Quantity Surveyors" as a separate professional organization is very common in the U.K.. This has, therefore, been promoted extensively outside the U.K. and used in many former British colonies. When Msaada Architects' clients have demanded, we use a "Bills of Quantities" on projects, though, this has usually resulted in higher construction costs. That is largely because the measured quantities also have several suggested inclusions for unforeseen expenses.

In fairness, though, while we in Msaada have not seen a benefit from using that system, it does provide another way to periodically cross-check the overall construction cost. Thus, doing so is likely often a main reason for using "Bills of Quantities" for implementation of building projects in the developing world by some organizations.

As an outgrowth of our initiated material procurement system, when Douglas Hincks oversaw Msaada Architects' Arusha area office, he created a kind of small "hardware store" in one bedroom of his house. This allowed him to supply hardware to smaller projects and to ensure that the surplus of hardware left over from larger projects was put to good use. Another benefit of having this "store" was that it increased our awareness about the importance of working with local, easily available materials as much as possible.

By having this material procurement program in the latter part of the 1980s, Msaada Architects ensured that many of our projects in Tanzania were completed when others had great difficulties accomplishing projects. As a result, Msaada's staff were at times asked to present at workshops for government employees regarding how we got projects implemented when others were mostly not able to do so at that time.

Challenging On-Site Experiences

Visiting the construction site of the new **Apartment Building in Iso-raka, Madagascar,** once gave me a sleepless night in Antananarivo. This was after I had arrived too late on the first day to go and properly visit the site for that project, which was being built on a steep hill just above the home of Madagascar's finance minister. Fortunately, my nightmare about how the new building could maybe slide down on top of the finance minister's house was fully put to rest when I was able to properly inspect construction the next day. We depended extensively on our local indigenous structural/civil engineer in the Madagascar area office to complete this project well and safely.

A bigger surprise for me in Madagascar happened when Msaada Architects' expat resident architect decided to add an attic floor to a new **Deaf Centre for the Lutheran Church in Antananarivo** after it was already under construction. He did this without checking with the home office and, to make matters worse, the structural design for this building had been done by somebody else on a site with serious foundation concerns because of a very high groundwater level.

Let me also mention that although I have always had a habit of not traveling overseas just to attend the opening ceremony for a new facility, I attended the inauguration for that Deaf Centre project as I was to be in the country, anyway. The Norwegian Minister of Aid to the Developing World was present for that event, and she surprised me by pointing out that there was a simple cross visible on one of the building's facades that was not supposed to be there.

This was created by using glass blocks in the masonry wall in the shape of a cross to take light into a small space used for prayers. This detail had not been included in the design, but it had been added during construction. Thus, it was quickly arranged to remove this simple, unobtrusive cross, and I made a personal apology to the Norwegian government's minister.

As head of Msaada Architects, the biggest challenge I have encountered on a site arose during the construction of a four-story, new **St. Cyprian's Anglican School in Maputo, Mozambique.** A Tanzanian architect who was sent there to serve as the project's Clerk of Works managed daily A/E construction observation and supervision. But periodically, he was visited by an expat structural/civil engineer in charge of our Tanzania area office at that time. That engineer was a missionary kid who had grown up in Tanzania, so he was expected to be culturally sensitive.

I was, therefore, very surprised to get a phone call one day from the General Secretary of DanChurchAid in Copenhagen, which funded the project. He told me how he had been contacted by the Anglican Bishop of Mozambique about a very unfortunate situation caused by Msaada Architects' expat engineer from the Tanzania office when he made a final site visit on his way back to the airport to return to Tanzania. Thus, DanChurchAid demanded that I find my way to Maputo to deal with that situation as quickly as possible. It didn't matter that I had never had a situation like this before (or since then) where I would have to travel overseas with only a day's notice.

Although Msaada Architects' expat engineer had been right to object to the very wet concrete he'd seen poured during his final site visit, he should have reacted in a more culturally sensitive manner. It was thus good to have the Anglican Bishop express, when I left after my visit to Maputo, how we all were now — to use a Henry Nouwen term, as he mentioned — "wounded healers." Even better, with help from the University of Maputo, it was possible to use a low-tech method to strength-test all reinforced concrete slabs. None of them failed those tests.

Importance of Services During Construction
Two very important examples of when it was essential for Msaada Architects to provide our own Clerk of Works for construction observation/supervision have been mentioned earlier. These were for **St.**

Timothy Lutheran Church in Bangui, Central African Republic, and for the large **ALC School Project in India.**

Msaada Architects has also had numerous examples where it was necessary to teach reluctant building contractors something new, only to later realize how rewarding it was afterward when such contractors were excited about their newly acquired skills. It was only when I was a missionary architect in Nigeria that I used my skills as a trained bricklayer to show how things were to be done if the construction workers objected to doing something that I knew rather easily could be shown to them as not being that complicated.

We also have had examples of how extensive involvement during the construction phase of projects can lead to cultural conflicts, such as when I was asked too frequently in India by the Arcot Lutheran Church to spend time attending functions for cornerstone laying or inaugurations of completed projects. Something that I, for practical reasons, simply had to limit to one such function every time I visited that church, but the Indian friends were not happy about that because of their desire to always show great hospitality. I, therefore, had to stress how my main objective in India was to help projects be implemented and not to attend functions, however nice or interesting those might be.

Especially for projects in Haiti, Msaada has often encountered financial donors who wanted — or almost demanded — to have U.S.-based building contractors do the construction of projects. While that might guarantee high-quality construction, it also results in higher construction costs. And it prevents local people from gaining the experience they need to build capacity and successfully complete additional development projects that arise in the future.

Thus, when a local Haitian building contractor, who had already worked on projects with Msaada Architects as the A/E, was challenged by the USAID about their qualifications, they almost lost their bid to build a new **Haitian Women's Prison.** So, they contacted us, and since this was the first local indigenous firm to be given a chance by USAID to be a building contractor on one of that organization's projects in

Haiti, Msaada agreed to be the A/E during the implementation of construction work.

We did this, although prisons are not exactly what Msaada Architects usually does! But that satisfied USAID, and the project was successfully completed. We were then also able to ensure important improvements in the project's design, which had been done by a U.S.-based A/E firm that probably knew a lot about prison designs in the U.S., but which seemingly was not that familiar with projects generally in Haiti.

Reflections regarding "Appropriate Technology"
Earlier, I described how using a staircase to join two three-story buildings for a new **Lutheran Centre in Moshi, Tanzania,** eliminated the need for elevators. This project also provided an example of when the economic and cultural impact of technology needed to be considered, for the building contractor inquired if he could get an imported crane as part of his payment for construction work. However, doing so would deprive scores of women from carrying the concrete used for this rather large, reinforced concrete/masonry structure.

So, although purchasing a large piece of equipment would have saved manual labor and construction time, it would have put many women out of work. Thus, when that was explained to the bishop, the request by the contractor was dropped by him. And while carrying concrete on their heads might not be ideal work for anybody, we needed to consider how these women often were the sole breadwinners for their families. So, they probably needed the work more urgently than some workers who manufactured building cranes somewhere in the Western world.

I might also add how, as I see it, the term "appropriate technology" has often been misused by many Western expatriates in the developing world when they have re-created (or reinvented) simple technology that already might have existed, even for a long time in the developing world.

So, appropriate technology in that part of the world is not always the lowest possible technology, as some Western expatriates in especially African countries often seem to believe. Instead, it is important to evaluate all aspects of what it might mean to decide to go forward with both less developed as well as with more advanced technology. The latter Msaada Architects certainly learned on the project for the new Lutheran Centre in Moshi, Tanzania.

Lutheran Deaf Centre, Antanarivo, Madagascar

St. Cyprian's Anglican School in Maputo, Mozambique

Haiti Women's Prison

CHAPTER 17

INTERACTION WITH OTHERS

M saada Architects has often accepted assignments to change and improve designs done by other architects who did not have sufficient experience for a specific project. And while it is rather common for architects and engineers in the Western world to do pro bono work for projects in the developing world, I have often heard expressed in Africa, how such services are not of much value, if the resulting designs are not appropriate for the functions that need to occur within a facility, are not related to the local climatic conditions, or are overdesigned structurally and thus usually also cost-prohibitive to build.

Therefore, as elsewhere, it is also in the developing world important to be ready to work with other building professionals as might be required. Msaada Architects has further had several experiences, where we were asked to interact with building professionals in some countries where the A/Es were lacking the knowledge and/or experience needed for implementing church-sponsored projects like those Msaada has for so long been accustomed to serving on.

Learning from the Wisdom of Others

It is Msaada Architects' experience that, by far, the best results for projects in the developing world come from the willingness of all stakeholders to learn from the wisdom of others. This does not mean getting as many people as possible involved with a project, as has often been suggested to us, seemingly so those involved will not be held individually responsible for decisions made. Such an approach will likely instead increase the cost of a project. But it does include the need, as often mentioned, for everybody involved to be culturally sensitive to where a project is located and who is going to use a new or renovated building.

We also recommend that specialized experts be involved as required, and as already has been suggested, that architects should listen with two big ears and speak with one small mouth when gathering information from a client at the time a project is initiated. Architects should especially ensure that those who will be using the planned new or renovated facility are heard. Everybody has something valuable to contribute if it is done upfront instead of when construction has commenced and costly "change orders" might be required.

Interaction With Other Building Professionals
A **Centre for a Lutheran Congregation in Novosibirsk, Russia,** was a project that entailed transforming an industrial building into something very different. It also required Msaada to teach the local Russian architects and engineers something new. So, a short Msaada visit resulted in a better design and the project being done within budget after the local architects and engineers were given information about the importance of those factors. Significant design changes happened already during my visit, resulting in a more inspiring worship space and other general improvements.

Another time I went to Russia was to advise on a project for **restoring a 300 year old Lutheran Church in St. Petersburg**. One of the teaching assignments I devised for architectural graduate students at the University of Minnesota explored whether to keep two reinforced concrete floor slabs in that church in place or to have them removed. These slabs were added during Soviet times when the church was used as a factory!

Keeping them gave more space for the local congregation to use for other activities than worship, and it further eliminated the risk of damaging the nearly 300-year-old building, which could occur if those slabs were removed as had been suggested by local consultants. And the worship space had originally been so tall that the top floor alone could now comfortably be used for this purpose.

Another example of Msaada Architects interacting with other building professionals was when we encountered very bad soil conditions for the earlier mentioned large project to rebuild **St. Francois de Sales Hospital in Port-au-Prince,** Haiti. It was rather late in the design process when we realized how exceedingly poor the bearing capacity of the soil was, mostly because of a high groundwater level. Thus, after both expat and indigenous geotechnical engineers in Port-au-Prince had proposed very expensive foundation designs to compensate for the poor soil condition, Msaada ended up using a much less expensive "ballasted soil foundation system" under all new two-story buildings.

That solution was proposed by an experienced geotechnical engineer who resided in the Twin Cities and who was recommended to us by our consulting structural engineer, after we had become rather desperate. We needed to build two-story instead of one-story buildings, as had been suggested by the hospital staff, because the project's total required floor area for new and renovated buildings was equal to the full site area. By using two-story buildings, half the site would be built upon, and the other half would be left as open, outside space (which was required).

Interaction With Client-Related Building Professionals

Msaada Architects has done several projects where we only provided services through the completion of construction documents. These projects usually involved a missionary builder taking control of construction implementation, and, fortunately, most of these experiences have been good.

However, there are also examples of how some things can go wrong. This was the case, for example, with the height of doors at the earlier mentioned **Kagando Baptist Hospital project in Uganda,** when a British missionary building engineer supervised construction work and unfortunately reduced the height of doors, making them definitely too low.

We also had a rather unusual experience with a restoration/improvement project in Germany involving turning an over 500-year-old building, which had originally been a boy's secondary school (Latin Schule) before it was now changed to be an **International Lutheran Welcome Centre in Wittenberg** for part of the German Lutheran Church.

Although we agreed to work with a local architect who was a member of that church, that did not work out so well. Thus, I personally had the difficult task of recommending that he be replaced with an architect who was not part of the local Lutheran Church but who had, importantly, completed several other restoration projects in Wittenberg. I was also responsible for getting this recommendation approved by the local church as well as by the donor church for the project in the U.S. (the Lutheran Church Missouri Synod).

It is also relevant to mention how Msaada often has worked with client representatives who were not building professionals but who had extensive experience with building projects. Such a person was the now late Rev. Stan Benson, who with his wife were fellow missionaries, when my wife and I served the national Tanzanian Lutheran Church in the 1970s. Stan and I worked together again later, after Msaada had become a reality.

Stan's letter at Msaada's 25th anniversary included the following excerpts after he had listed some of the assistance he'd received from Msaada on building projects in his role as project coordinator for the diocese he served: **"As we are all brothers in the mission of the church there is little difference between your local MSAADA staff and those of the diocese....... MSAADA will always have work as more churches, schools, and medical facilities are needed."**

Interaction With Other Client-Related Persons

A small but very interesting project that involved interaction with several people who had different opinions was the initial phase of the new **Quo Vadis Centre in Tamil Nadu, India.** This is a centre for religious dialogue between Christians, Hindus, and Muslims. It not only serves Indians but also reaches out to the approximately 500 Westerners, who usually are in that city at any given time because of its large and famous Hindu temple, as well as a mountain to circumnavigate, which is considered very holy by Hinduism.

In the earlier chapter about the **ALC School Project in India,** I mentioned how I had collaborated with an educational sociologist when doing a feasibility study and preparing a pilot project proposal. That person suggested the importance of having an in-service teachers' training program, as well as ensuring that equipment and learning materials were available in remodeled or new school buildings. Everything regarding the design of classrooms was later discussed with staff in the project's educational component.

Working in as many countries as Msaada Architects has worldwide given me the opportunity to meet many intriguing people, most of whom have been normal, average people. But I have also had the opportunity to meet well-known significant church leaders worldwide, plus some other dignitaries. As an example, my wife and I met and talked for quite some time with Johnny Cash and his wife, June Carter, about a hospital project in Kenya, which they supposedly were to support financially.

It is unfortunate, though, how that project never materialized for reasons I have never been able to truly understand. That is especially so because of the hard work done by the driving force behind the project — a person who was both Johnny Cash's spiritual advisor and his friend. But also due to the involvement in fundraising by so well-known people as the Cash/Carter's.

However, for me personally, the most important persons I have met in the developing world have been the many indigenous church leaders and other committed and serious Christians, whom I have seen sacrifice so much for their faith. Something which has repeatedly made me aware of how, in so many ways, it seemingly is much easier to be a Christian believer in the Western World than in many other parts of the world. And something which repeatedly has been an inspiration for me about what it should involve, at least as I understand it, for us who hope to "qualify" as being called Christians, to truly give our best to act on what Jesus the Christ asks of us.

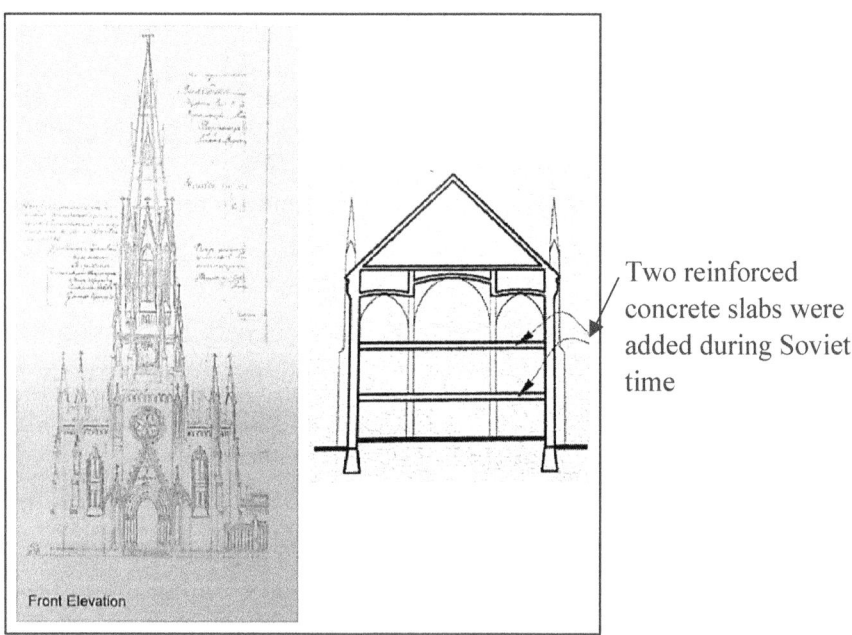

Two reinforced concrete slabs were added during Soviet time

Front Elevation

Restoration of an old Lutheran Church in St. Petersburg, Russia

International Lutheran Welcome Centre in Wittenberg, Germany

Quo Vadis Centre in Tamil Nadu, India

CHAPTER 18

PROJECTS IN THE U.S.

Msaada Architects has done a few projects in the U.S., mostly after the turn of the last millennium. That was, after all, the Northern European church-related donor organizations simultaneously decided to concentrate on programs in the developing world rather than brick-and-mortar projects. Up until that time, these organizations had provided for Msaada Architects the large majority of the projects we had served on in the developing world.

Most of the projects handled in this country by Msaada Architects have been church buildings, which is in line with what the organization can legally do for other nonprofits. Our involvement with such projects resulted from articles in a couple of Lutheran publications, which stated how Msaada was ready to provide A/E services on some projects for congregations here in the U.S.

After having seen such projects implemented, we became busy again in the developing world and returned to focusing on that. This happened partly because we in Msaada had initiated the funding programs for projects in the developing world, which were included in the earlier mentioned "**Project Opportunities for Interested Financial Partners.**"

Sample Projects
The projects we saw implemented in the U.S. included not only the earlier mentioned new home for the **Lutheran Church in Faulkton,**

South Dakota, but also projects that materialized for three other congregations in that state. Those included two projects, which involved remodeling and expansion of existing facilities. Related to that, I personally find that projects to improve and expand existing church facilities in the Western world can often be even more meaningful for an architect than to design something completely new.

The value of that was affirmed in two additional implemented projects in South Dakota, which involved improvements and expansion of **St. John's Lutheran Church in Hot Springs,** for which we received the following message from the Chair of the Building Committee: **"Thank you for your interest in St. John's as a people and not as just a building project. Your efforts to help us build a mission for Christ have shown through constantly."**

It further included improvements and expansion of **Custer Lutheran Church,** and the following is a message from the pastor received while the project was still under construction: **"Things are progressing well. Thank you for your excellent leadership, your ability to work with people, your understanding of design issues, and your love for the church."**

Msaada did a few other church projects in Minnesota and in Wisconsin, which in the latter state included a new church home for **Trinity Lutheran Church in McKinley.** Other projects in those two states were smaller remodeling projects of existing church facilities.

It seems relevant here to focus on a message received from the pastor of **Stanfold Lutheran Church in Wisconsin.** For that message emphasized the "Sharing the Blessings" program, which Msaada initiated around the year 2000: **"Thank you again for your time in coming all this way to visit. And thank you for your mission both as it touches us here in Northwest Wisconsin, but more importantly, as it builds up the body of Christ in much more challenged areas of the world.**

Importantly note, though, how a small **expansion of a Medical Missionaries of Mary facility in a suburb of Boston, Massachusetts,** may make it easier to understand why Msaada Architects even earlier had gone beyond only doing projects in the developing world, for this was our first U.S. project. We did it upon request from Sr. Margaret O'Conor, who oversaw the first project Msaada completed, which was at the **Makiungu Roman Catholic Hospital in Tanzania.**

When Margaret called me about the proposed project in the Greater Boston Area, I naturally responded with how I believed she understood we did not serve on projects in the U.S., only for me to get the quick response from her: **"But you do so now!"**

So, after having done the project in the Greater Boston Area plus later those for congregations here in the Upper Midwest, we also agreed to do small, limited projects for not only the Minnesota Church Center in Minneapolis, Minnesota (where our offices were located for more than a decade), but also for **Luther Park Camping and Retreat Center** in Wisconsin. When the latter project was completed, we received the following brief note from the Director of the Center: **"I really enjoyed working with all of you in Msaada. You do excellent work."**

Msaada also did a small extension of the **Danish American Center in Minneapolis**. That was possible, as it also was for another nonprofit. Since Msaada is a registered nonprofit organization, at least 90% of our projects must legally be for other nonprofits as has been mentioned earlier.

We have, though, also done a few projects within the 10% allowed for other organizations. Those have also been in the U.S. primarily, and therefore not in other parts of the world, and they have mostly been single-family houses for people whom we had already been involved with related to projects in the developing world.

However, our total involvement with projects in the U.S. totals significantly less than the 10% that we could have done for organizations that are not nonprofit, even when other nonprofit projects we have served on in this country are also included in the total of U.S. projects, which we have seen implemented.

Custer Lutheran Church in South Dakota

Trinity Lutheran Church in McKinley, WI

Luther Park Camping and Retreat Center in WI

Danish American Center in Minneapolis

PART FIVE

LESSONS LEARNED

CHAPTER 19

COLLABORATION

The opportunity to work and serve with people in many different cultures is a major reason why I, for so long, have continued to enjoy and much appreciate what I have been so richly blessed to do for many years as an architect in the developing world. The value of working with and collaborating with numerous people of different racial and ethnic backgrounds than my own has enriched my life tremendously.

Collaboration With Building Contractors

I have always considered it important for A/E's to be ready to collaborate well with building contractors and their staff instead of those two parties looking upon each other as adversaries, as often seems to be the case in this country. As mentioned earlier, it is also important throughout a project that the architect, as well as any involved building engineers, continue to keep in mind that a project belongs to the client and not to those who have been assigned to plan, design, and implement it. Keeping that in mind also assists in viewing projects holistically, so to speak, within their larger real-world contexts.

Msaada Architects has, therefore, always had as an additional goal to not only teach new skills to the building contractors in the developing world but, as importantly, to cooperate rather extensively with them. It is at least my experience that the best results are obtained in building projects anywhere if the expertise and experience of the A/Es are combined with those of the building contractors and their workers as much as possible.

For that reason, Msaada has often involved the building contractors in conversations about which details to use and, of no less importance, about what kind of fixtures to use. Their construction experiences related to what their workers know best will greatly benefit the project; and furthermore, these contractors also know how to get the best possible products for the best possible price.

An important example of this was when it had been planned to use flush doors on a large project in India, and the building contractor suggested that wooden panel doors be used instead. To my reply stating how such doors usually are more expensive, the building contractor replied that was not the case for him, as his craftsmen were used to making such doors so that they would be cheaper and of better quality for the project than flush doors. So, a win-win situation was achieved.

Msaada has on many other projects, also involved the building contractor at an early stage in the design process regarding which materials and details to use to get the best possible solution with the most value for the money spent. In addition, we have, more often than not, when tender/bid results have come in higher than expected, used the opportunity to discuss with the lowest bidder how the budget might be reached without sacrificing the quality of construction by, for example, using detailing or materials which might be examples of "six of one or half a dozen of another," to ensure that the quality of "the final product" is not sacrificed while the cost was reduced to meet a required budget.

A prime example of a project that had quite extensive design involvement by the building contractors and their foremen or engineers was, as earlier mentioned **Chapel project in India** which required several such chapels to be built for the Arcot Lutheran Church. Because it was designed by us in Msaada with extensive use of detailing, etc., from Hindu Temples, it further became an example where we uniquely allowed for different interpretations of some of the detailing, thereby giving the building contractors and their engineers or foremen an even stronger feeling that the final "product" was truly influenced by them. As a definite fringe benefit, this involvement then also resulted in the built chapels not entirely looking alike but instead with each having an individual identity.

That project also initially included a suggestion to perhaps let the chapels influence matters related to worship by making, for example, the altar table lower so the pastor might sit on it in the fashion of how Indian leaders often sit cross-legged in front of gatherings. However, that proposal was not accepted by the then Bishop of the ALC.

However, a pastor who later became the ALC bishop wrote the following about one of the chapels built in that project: **"The church in Vadalur, which was built in Indian style and inaugurated in 1988, is in constant dialogue with people of other faiths...This structure, with an architectural detailing of the broader religious India, is a "signboard" for the Arcot Lutheran Church. It invites discussions inside and outside the church about the necessity for dialogue and content in evangelism in the midst of the multi-religious Indian subcontinent."**

Msaada Architects could not have asked for a stronger affirmation that the intentions behind the design of this facility as well as other chapels built in that project had been met or maybe even exceeded related to both objectives of creating Cristian places for worship with Indian inspired designs, but also with having rather extensive involvement of the local building contractors and their staff.

Collaboration With Associate Architects and Engineers

The first major attempt for Msaada in working more broadly with other local architectural and engineering firms in the developing world, after the experience in India working with an associate architect, was when the organizations Africa area offices around the change of the last millennium were replaced with associate offices. Some of these collaborations worked well, while some did not. Thus, Msaada has again periodically realized a need to have staff stationed for shorter periods of time in countries where it earlier had its own offices. Stationing staff in these countries is done to support the associate offices in meeting the needs of the clients, and it is usually only done upon special client requests.

A project for a new **Lutheran Town Clinic in Arusha, Tanzania**, is an example, though, of how Msaada giving up its own office in a country resulted in us later not getting to do a larger medical project for a client we already had served extensively earlier. The client was not satisfied with the services provided by our associate architect's office during the construction of this project and, therefore, did not want us to do a next larger medical project in the same location. That was a great disappointment, but a reality we had to deal with, meaning also that we found another associate architectural firm in Tanzania.

In countries where Msaada does not have an associate office, we always expect to have an A/E of record for the projects the organization is asked to serve on. That has, in some situations, as in the former Soviet Union, also given local A/E's opportunities to learn more and expand their horizons. Further, it has reduced Msaada's need to deal too much with local authorities and not needing excessive research regarding which local materials and building technologies are appropriate for a given project.

On a very large project for a new proposed **National Referral Hospital in Singida, Tanzania**, Msaada suggested and got acceptance from the client for an arrangement where we did the concept designs and the design development, leaving the production of construction documents in the hands of instructors at architectural and engineering universities and colleges in Tanzania.

The important idea was that architectural students, as well as students in the various engineering disciplines — civil, structural, mechanical, and electrical, as well as surveying, etc. — would learn from working on that project. Instead, the local instructors did their part of the design work in their private offices/studios. That was unfortunate, as the opportunity of having students work on and learn from a large project like this, which was to be implemented in the real world, was then lost.

For a long time, Msaada was fortunate to have a very experienced Architect/Structural Engineer on staff part-time doing structural design in the Minnesota office. In the countries where Msaada had its own offices, the local engineers in those offices usually did at least part of the structural engineering designs. In India, our associate office always used an associate engineer of theirs for structural designs.

When the combined Architect/Structural Engineer in Msaada's home office retired, arrangements were made to have an associate U.S. structural engineer involved, and that arrangement worked extremely well for many years on numerous projects. Further, we have also periodically worked with an associate U.S. civil engineer as well as a U.S. geo-tech engineer.

However, when some projects in Haiti also required assistance from U.S. registered mechanical and electrical engineers, Msaada had a hard time, at first, finding a firm to cooperate with. Before I explain this further, I should note that on most projects, Msaada expects that architects on staff can also do basic mechanical and electrical engineering designs for projects in the developing world.

But when we needed a U.S. mechanical and electrical engineering firm to cooperate with on a regular basis, the main obstacle we encountered with some firms was that they wanted to "tell us what they thought was needed" instead of listening to what was truly required. For what is needed in the developing world is mostly quite different from what might be required in the U.S. Thus, if we had listened to those engineers' suggestions, mechanical and electrical systems would have been over-designed and exceeded the budget, which, in the worst-case scenarios, might financially have "killed" the projects.

Fortunately, we did find a firm doing mechanical and electrical designs that listened to what was needed, and they could also do the work for the fees available. So, later projects done together with them in other countries beyond Haiti have been carried out with their fees being within the not-to-exceed cost for mechanical and electrical designs.

Well-Meaning but Questionable Assistance

Msaada has tried to have a few retired architects and engineers involved as volunteers, but that has mostly not turned out so well, primarily because volunteers are not always ready to do things when they need to be done. There has, though, for a long time been much interest from Americans to volunteer to go to Africa for building projects on very short-term trips of maybe just a couple of weeks, even if they are not building professionals or skilled craftsmen and, thus, should be considered unskilled labor for building work there.

I naturally have reservations about such arrangements, except for specialized work when there are no local experts available, for there are plenty of capable craftsmen in Africa who need the work that such volunteers take away from them. There is no comparison between the cost of using African labor and the cost of work done by such visitors if the cost of traveling to Africa for maybe just a couple of weeks of work is also included. That also means people in the developing world are expected to submit to a kind of indignity in exchange for assistance from the Western World. Something which the late Mwalimu Nyerere rightly warned against, as has been mentioned earlier.

There are, though, also examples of people going on so-called *mission trips* (which should be called *vision trips,* I believe) without skills for assisting with a building project, who returned to the U.S. as great ambassadors for what is happening in the developing world. That is, of course, always valuable, and often results in others also starting to support meaningful projects.

Msaada has periodically also sent an expat to serve overseas to get one or more projects done, but that has usually been to work as a Building Supervisor/Clerk of Works, and instead of that person being in the country for a week or two, we talk about months or even a year or two. Jeff Potts was such a person, and he wrote to me after having been in Uganda for some months to share what he thought about persons from the U.S. going to Africa for a short time and calling themselves "missionaries." He stated they likely learned more themselves and were instead evangelized to by the Africans.

Jeff wrote further: "People here have been thoroughly saturated with "hit-and-run missionaries" who throw money at them, snap a picture to show their friends, then run off to the nearest game reserve looking for flushing toilets and hand sanitizer. This fake "mission work" has greatly offended the Ugandans' dignity and caused them to turn charity into something of a game."

Additionally, he wrote about how he had learned the need for him to be patient with the Ugandans, as they needed to see if he was a "fake," or a "real" mission worker. Thus, he stated "as a way of testing you, to see if you really care about them, they will frustrate the daylights out of you by taking what we Americans value most — our time." After some additional info about what he had learned from that, he then reached the point where, as he stated, some of them began to be honest with me and trust me enough to let me teach them and learn from them. The best investment we from America are making in Uganda is not our money; it's our wasted time. For people here are watching."

I appreciated receiving that information from Jeff about what he experienced as a very observant young architectural graduate serving in Africa for about a year, for I have seen some of the same in many developing countries, but I have mostly avoided stating this as directly as Jeff did to me. However, I have, especially in Haiti, seen too many groups from Church congregations or other organizations coming from the U.S. for a short time believing they serve the local population, while they instead often do more damage by creating dependency among the local population instead of assisting with capacity building.

Church in Vadalur in Chapel Project for Arcot Lutheran Church, in India

Lutheran Town Clinic in Arusha, Tanzania

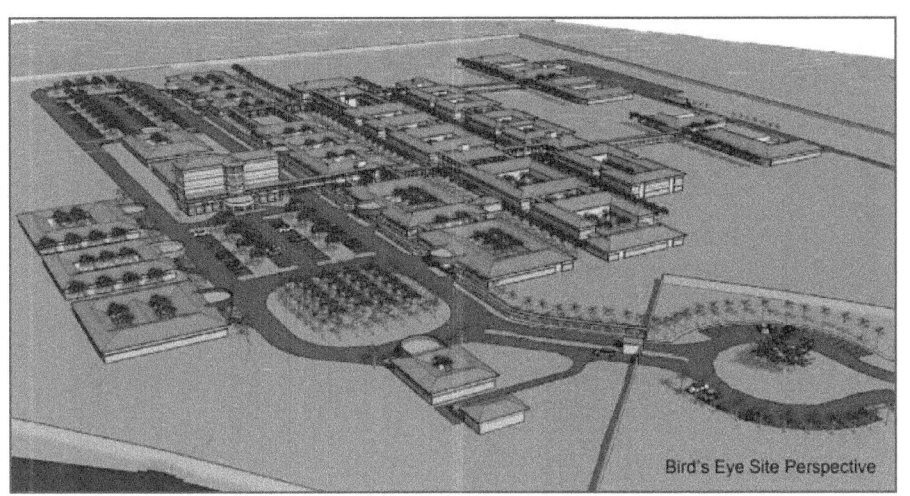

Bird's Eye Site Perspective

National Referral Hospital in Singida, Tanzania

CHAPTER 20

HAVING THE RIGHT STAFF

Msaada Architects' work has always required having committed, high-quality staff, which, perhaps, should have been expected to be complicated to recruit, considering how the organization has always only been able to pay by Western standards **less than average salaries for beyond average productivity**. This is something that I have always stressed upfront in interviews with potential new staff to help avoid misunderstandings about what can be expected financially when working for Msaada.

This policy, or requirement, is based on the relatively low salaries Msaada Architects has been able to pay and on an expectation that those interested in serving through an organization such as Msaada should understand how doing exciting and meaningful work also means getting reduced monetary compensation. For at least as I see it, this is balanced by the many "intrinsic" rewards from providing A/E services for building projects in the developing world which help to ensure that required facilities for providing life-enhancing services for our global neighbors are being designed and getting built.

Staff in the Home Office

As indicated already, finding the correct staff to serve in Msaada's home office as well as to work in one of our area offices as an expat was not that complicated for a long time. The best way to illustrate how former and present staff reacted to what was expected earlier and what their experiences were like might be by sharing excerpts from just a few of the letters received from former and present staff, at the 25th anniversary in 2005.

Thus, I will initially mention Scott Williams, who joined Msaada Architects in 1986, when he was the first person to become in charge of an overseas office without initially having worked for a couple of years in Msaada's Minnesota office. Scott was doing so partly because he already had a few years of experience and was also already a certified architect in this country. But it was further because we did not have anybody else in the home office who had the expected two years of experience with us in that office before going overseas to head up an area office.

Fortunately, it turned out so that when Scott had spent three years overseas, first in the Madagascar area office in Antananarivo and later in the office in Nairobi, Kenya, he was ready to return to the Minnesota home office to be Studio Chief. That was a position I had filled until then, besides being Executive Director and Principal Architect. Juggling three roles had become almost too much after the home office had been supplemented with three Africa area offices and an associate office in India. Scott and I have both been blessed and mutually inspired professionally to work extremely well together up until we both retired towards the end of 2019, when the home office was moved to Findlay, Ohio.

Scott began his letter at the time of Msaada's 25th anniversary by first telling how he was not really looking for a job at the time when he joined Msaada, but that if he had the opportunity to do what Msaada Architects might offer, he was ready to take off for Madagascar, and this is what he did. He then added in his anniversary letter: **"Now, nearly 20 years later, I'm grateful and even more fortunate that I joined MSAADA ...Since then, MSAADA's projects have taken me to initially Madagascar but later also to other countries in Africa and Asia.**

Scott closes his letter with the following comments reflecting on what Msaada Architects had been able to be involved with during its then-initial 25 years of existence: **"It is amazing that we have been successfully making such a difference in the lives of the poor for 25 years now, Poul. There are so many projects built, and so many lives have changed. I am thankful that my life is also one of those touched by MSAADA."**

As mentioned, Scott continued to work for Msaada until the end of 2019, when I retired as Executive Director, and he is still working as a design consultant to the organization after W. Jerry Murray took over my position and I became a general consultant. So, both of us are now involved only in Msaada as might be required, needed or desired by the executive director.

Many former staff architects who have gone on to do other work sent their reflections for our 25th Anniversary celebration. Here is an excerpt from Jason Krumm's letter: **"When I first contacted Poul, little did I know that my correspondence with him would last two years because of the disruptions related to the Sept. 11, 2001, event. But it was certainly worth the wait!"**

Jason left Msaada partly because we could not meet his wish for the organization to be more involved in South America, where he had a personal interest. But he included the following comment in his letter: **"Though I know I am no longer officially a part of the MSAADA team, I find myself talking about the work, the mission, and the projects almost daily." When closing the letter, he stated: "What rich, full, and challenging years these now 25 years have been for MSAADA! Being a part of the MSAADA Team was and is a big part of my identity."**

Here is a brief quote from Elizabeth Forslund, for whom architecture was a second career after having been a teacher for some years: **"The 5+ years I spent at MSAADA were the most interesting and enjoyable of my architectural career."**

Patricia Mestenhauser Bergh worked for us as an architect for a couple of decades, initially as a single person. Later, when she married, she worked off and on during the time she and her husband raised their family. Her 25th Anniversary message describes how, early on, she went to Kenya for a short time, and it closes with how she at that time saw Msaada Architects: **"What began with dreams and prayers of a handful of people in a small corner of the world has been sustained all these years by the dreams and prayers of thousands of people throughout the world. I am one of the thousands who have been touched by MSAADA through my dreams and prayers."**

With numerous architectural graduates having worked in our offices over the years, it is impossible to refer to the large majority of them. But here is what Scott Lundberg stated shortly: **"Thank you for one of the most professional experiences I have had."**

After she left us, Beth Evanson Makhoul shared the following: **"I worked for MSAADA as recently as the end of 2016. Before that, I had Poul as a professor at the University of Minnesota Architectural program in the 'Building Stories' course."**

As somebody who worked for us for a rather long time without being an architectural graduate (but who'd CAD at Dunwoody College of Technology in Minneapolis), Tim Helmeke stated: **"On a bus ride, I talked with a woman who used to work for an architectural firm called MSAADA, which specialized in doing projects in mostly Africa and India. That really caught my interest, and now, after five years working for MSAADA, I love what the organization stands for and what I have learned."**

While it is essential to have the right A/E staff, it is also important to have the right clerical support staff. So here are excerpts from an anniversary letter by Marian Kyllo, who served extremely well as my "right-hand person" in administrative matters for a decade until she was ready to retire: **"I went to work part-time for MSAADA as Secretary/Administrative Assistant...I stayed for ten years."** Marian later added: **"There were so many dedicated young men and women who** were willing and ready to go to Africa to enable MSAADA to get the work done."

Beverly Meakins followed Marian as the administrative assistant in our Minnesota office. Here, she describes the value of Msaada Architects' work as she saw it: **"Theme is transformation, and MSAADA's work is about international transformation of people who have worked with MSAADA to create something good for those they do not even know. And it is about transformation of a building ("external") which provides internal transformation for people's lives and their own hopes for their future."**

Erica Boyles also served Msaada as a young clerical staff person, and, based on that experience, she decided to go back to study to become an architect. She described in a letter for me with some frustration one of her earlier days of studying architecture: **"As I drove home, however, your words echoed in my mind: 'Never lose your enthusiasm and idealism.' And I then realized that no matter how much time I will spend learning architecture theory, I will always adhere to what I learned at MSAADA: that good design and quality construction don't need to be expensive. That it's important to design culturally and geographically appropriate structures. And, most importantly, that architecture, above all else, is about serving others — in particular, others who have so much less than we have financially."**

It is encouraging that after recent years, when it became harder to find staff wanting to serve based on Msaada Architects' criteria, this might be changing now when the younger generations represent about half of the global workforce. For many of these demographic groups, the focus is on doing something meaningful. Thus, they might provide future staff for Msaada and other A/E firms working for and serving in the developing world.

Expatriate Staff in Overseas Offices

In our Africa area offices, Msaada has always used indigenous local staff as extensively as possible. But when those offices were initiated, we started out with an expat architectural graduate in charge. That was usually somebody who first had worked for at least two years in our Minnesota office. The first such person was W. Jerry Murray, who opened the initial Msaada area office in Africa in late 1980 in Arusha, Tanzania. Jerry later moved to Kenya to open an area/regional office in Nairobi.

The following is an excerpt from a letter Msaada Architects received from Jerry for our 25th Anniversary in 2005: **"I had always dreamed of being an architect. By the time I entered college, I dreamed of building great works of art, being published, and winning awards for my genius. But then I met MSAADA. Suddenly, architecture was about shelter, service, and stewardship."**

In 1982, Douglas Hincks became the first civil/structural engineer in the Arusha, Tanzania office. Later, when Jerry Murray went to Nairobi to start the office there, Douglas was put in charge of the Tanzania office. Here is an excerpt from the letter he sent for the 25th anniversary: **"MSAADA was a life-changing episode in my life that lasted over eight years — from 1982 to 1990. Without a doubt, my experience with MSAADA has been the most fulfilling and rewarding work experience in my career."**

And here are excerpts from a letter, which was sent by Verle Hansen after he had spent only about half of a year in the Tanzania area office to assist with a busy project schedule: **"How do you take something from the natural environment to sustain human life and leave the environment intact? My Ph.D. work centered on this question, and it still occupies nearly all my research. Thank you, Poul, for the experiences in Africa that have led me in this direction!"**

Peter Ozolins started the area office in Antananarivo, Madagascar, as our second Africa area office, and here is what he wrote to us in 2005: **"As a young architect with a few years' experience in commercial and residential practice, I had already decided to abandon my** chosen profession to explore a career in linguistics owing to my disappointment with a profession that I found to be self-serving and only marginally concerned with matters of real importance to people's lives."

Peter then proceeds to explain how he learned about Msaada and what he did in his years in Madagascar, and later for a few years in Tanzania before he finishes with: **"This life-changing experience has defined me as a person and as an architect and still informs my work today."** A couple of years ago, we were extremely sad to learn that Peter's life and later work as a professor of architecture had unfortunately been cut short by an automobile accident.

Royce Wiens, who was later the resident architect in charge of the Madagascar office, shared these thoughts in an anniversary letter, too: **"It has been a privilege for you and I, Poul, to be part of what God has done through MSAADA; all the glory goes to God."**

Terry Piech, a female architect, was in charge of our Kenya office at one point. That was when she was already living in Nairobi because of her husband's job there and after she had worked for some time assisting the resident architect before her. I initially wondered, though, how Terry would handle that role in a male-dominated society. My concerns were put fully to rest when I observed her perform extremely well on a construction site for a complicated project being done also with a very challenging client representative.

Local Staff in Overseas Offices

Msaada Architects has always been blessed to have had very good indigenous local staff in our overseas offices. An example of the value of having local staff in Msaada Architects' area offices is the roof structure that needed to be put in place atop a new **Roman Catholic Church in Loruvani,** Tanzania. Aziz Moshi, our local structural engineer then in our Tanzania area office, "saved the day" by getting for this project a complicated and extremely heavy roof structure properly put in place without the use of a crane. This was after I had expressed my concern whether that could happen safely, as cranes are not common on building sites in Africa except for multi-story buildings in large cities.

In our Msaada Madagascar office, the most important local staff person was Jacquelin Randrianirina. He sent us at Msaads's 25th anniversary, a greeting which included the following excerpt: **"Since I have been with MSAADA, we have done about 150 projects around Madagascar, including missionary houses, church department offices, schools, dispensaries, hospitals, and church buildings, and I have had unlimited opportunities to live my faith through my work."**

It is appropriate to also mention how Peter Ozolins, as the person initially in charge of our Madagascar area office, once indicated to me that while he might be what we called the "resident architect" in the Antananarivo office, Jacquelin was the "resident angel."

Staffing Challenges and Successes

For Msaada Architects, it has always been most beneficial to employ Western A/E design staff, who are "not yet too set in their ways" from working in the Western world. Once, however, we needed somebody to take over as resident architects in two Africa area offices, so we hired two experienced architects for this. Both were recommended after they had run their own offices in their home countries, the U.S. and Denmark. But neither of them could reduce the amount of time they were accustomed to investing in the early stages of design. Thus, they were both let go due to dire financial reasons.

It was not so complicated to replace the one in the area office in Arusha, Tanzania, due primarily to its solid local support staff. But in contrast, it was challenging to replace the other one, as he had overseen the development of an office in Addis Ababa, Ethiopia, after a rather large project load had been secured in that country by efforts from our Minnesota and Kenya offices' staff. Unfortunately, the result was that we had to close the Ethiopia area office when the expatriate U.S. architect was let go.

There are also a few examples of young architects who could not get used to Msaada Architects' way of working either when they went overseas, usually after the two years of training and preparation in the Minnesota office. So, we also had to let them go. However, fortunately, most young architects adapted extremely well, and while they later left Msaada Architects, they had obtained skills they could also use elsewhere.

So, we are happy about having seen many examples of former Western architectural and engineering staff whose careers continued successfully afterward in their home countries, mostly the U.S., with several of the architects ending up with their own practices. That also affirms the value of what they had learned from working for Msaada. Further, at least a couple of our former U.S. staff members later became professors of architecture. And a few of our early expat staff members in our Africa area offices did stay on to continue working successfully overseas after they left us.

Finally, there are also very important examples of local staff in our Africa area offices who later became successful independent private practice architects or engineers in their home countries on that continent.

CHAPTER 21

CAPACITY BUILDING

As a natural follow-up of the previous chapter, allow me to reiterate how one of the many important things I have learned during my years of serving in the developing world as an expatriate has been to always be keenly aware of participating in capacity building of the indigenous population in the countries where projects are located. For only then can true development happen beyond just getting present building projects done. This also makes it easier for developing countries to become more self-reliant.

Self-Reliance and Capacity Building
When I served in the national Lutheran Church's central office in Tanzania, the key phrase related to proper development for a then rather recently independent country like Tanzania was "self-reliance." The "Fundi Training Program" mentioned earlier, which we developed, became a response to that — even though this program was initiated mainly to create much-required significant savings in construction cost for the large project for which it was used initially.

Being a person up there in age now, I often recall what an indigenous instructor at a Technical College in Tanzania said to me after I had started teaching part-time a half-spring semester graduate class at the School of Architecture at the University of Minnesota. He was no "spring chicken" either, and he suggested how he saw it as being "almost criminal" if persons like him and I go to our graves with all the professional knowledge we have accumulated without first passing that on to the younger generations to the extent possible. This book is, therefore, also a response to that suggestion to me by a true African "mzee" (Swahili for an older, wise person).

Unfortunately, earlier attempts by Msaada Architects to be further involved with teaching new A/E's outside our offices in more formal ways in the countries where the organization has served have not been successful. We have, though, always been aware of the importance of ensuring that local staff in our overseas offices develop skills that are useful not only when working for Msaada Architects but also when they might go and work elsewhere. So, we have never discouraged staff in our offices from moving on and working elsewhere because that extends the value of our presence in their country.

Thus, when the decision was made around the turn of the last millennium for Msaada Architects to no longer have its own area offices in Tanzania, Madagascar, and Kenya, the private firms with whom we had periodically collaborated in Tanzania and Kenya naturally became associated offices. Since our area office in Madagascar didn't have a private firm, which it had worked with earlier, the local indigenous staff asked if they could continue to work as kind of a franchise of Msaada Architects, although without having to pay a fee for this to our organization. That request was naturally accepted.

More recently, when the person who had set up the Haiti area office shortly after the earthquake in 2010, Andrew Ripp, wanted to return to the U.S., we did not send another expat to replace him. Instead, we asked Euvodine Exantus-Jean, who was already living in Haiti with a Jamaican passport, but with Haitian parents, to take over responsibility for that office. She earned her architectural degree in Jamaica, and she had by that time worked several years as a very capable assistant architect to Andrew.

Education of New Building Professionals

In the U.S., Msaada Architects' efforts to share our extensive experiences with future architects and building engineers included, for some years, providing a concept design project for a team of senior-year engineering students from various disciplines to work on at **Gonzaga Roman Catholic University in Spokane,** Washington. My co-teaching for almost a decade, a yearly half-semester graduate course at the **University of Minnesota's School of Architecture** in the College of Design, was also an important part of those efforts.

In connection with the latter assignment, I was also asked to be part of a small group developing a proposed new master's degree program with a focus on Public Interest Design, which was to result in that program becoming available online to persons in the developing world for a minimal cost. This was a program that also was to be geared more towards the work that the students hopefully would do after graduation, which would thus also involve more exposure to construction and to the building trades.

Having an understanding and maybe even some training and experience as a craftsman is something I believe is helpful for any architect. It has been extremely helpful for me in my work that I also passed the test to become a bricklayer craftsman in order to earn my diploma (as mentioned earlier, which is now called a bachelor's degree in Denmark).

That was after I had used mostly summer months, during the five years needed after High School graduation to complete the diploma program, to work as a bricklayer apprentice. Something which proved valuable already during my early 4+ years as an architect in my home country, but even more so later in Africa. I often wonder how I, without that experience, would have handled my later work in the developing world.

Thus, providing future architects with at least some building trade exposure might be a good thing to consider as part of their overall training in the U.S. This also supports the idea that architecture — as I see it — is "kunsthaandwaerk." Many colleagues might disagree —even in my home country — with me using that term for architecture, which is a Danish word that joins the two words for "art" and "crafts" into just one word, meaning **"artsy craft**." It is thus interesting for me to also have learned recently how some U.S. schools of architecture have started requiring some experience with building trade work to obtain an architectural degree.

Through my assignment as the only non-faculty person in the group developing the earlier mentioned planned new master's degree program at the University of Minnesota's School of Architecture, I learned how things at a university can move much more slowly than what I am used to from working as a practicing architect on projects in the developing world. They also move more slowly when compared to the work I did in the initial years of my career in Denmark for a well-established and growing architectural firm. So, eventually, I dropped out of that group as things continued to be delayed. I'm thus unsure what the result of that proposed program might have been.

However, despite the comments just made, I much enjoyed and greatly valued my teaching opportunities at the University of Minnesota, which allowed me to provide information about important matters to architectural graduate-level students. And later, Scott Williams was involved for a full academic year assisting one of the students attending Dunwoody College's new Bachelor of Architecture program in Minneapolis.

Also note, as was mentioned earlier, how it was not successful when, after completing design concepts and design development, Msaada Architects turned a project for the proposed **Fifth National Referral Hospital in Singida, Tanzania**, over to indigenous instructors at the national educational facilities of architectural and engineering faculties. For they ended up working on the A/E designs in their own local studios, and that was certainly not what was expected or what had been agreed upon with the project's client, represented by the governor of the Singida region in Tanzania. So, what seemed like a good idea was lost mostly because of the self-interest of the local instructors, and this approach did not end up benefiting students as had, importantly, been intended.

Local Associate Offices
One important way of supporting self-reliance and capacity building in the developing world is to establish and cooperate with local associate offices. As already mentioned, Msaada Architects has done this in India from when we first started serving on the ALC School Project. We made that arrangement largely out of necessity, though, as it was simply at that time impossible to get a resident permit for a Westerner in India.

So, the only solution seemed to be to collaborate with a local Architectural firm. Initially, it proved to be a great challenge to find the right firm. At first, we worked for about a year with one local firm, but this collaboration was not so successful. Later, when a local church worker in Madras (now Chennai) put us in contact with J. Inbaraaj Consultants, this turned out to be a true blessing, for the cooperation with that firm has always worked extremely well and has been mutually beneficial.

Thus, it is also relevant to quote here the following excerpts from a letter that Msaada Architects and I received from the owner of that firm, Jesudiaan Inbaraaj, for our 25th Anniversary: "**Down the memory lane about two decades ago...I believe it was God's plan that we met and established our association...I pray to God to bless you and MSAADA at this time of 25th anniversary.**"

So, when Msaada Architects later began using associate offices in Africa instead of having our own area offices there, the model of collaboration was largely based on the working situation in India between J. Inbaraaj Consultants and Msaada Architects. While the experiences regarding such arrangements in Africa have been mixed, this is now how the organization still mostly has served on that continent. I should further mention how Inbaraaj, unfortunately, died by the end of 2022. I, therefore, personally lost not only a close professional colleague and associate with whom I had worked together for so many years to our great mutual benefit and for the benefit of our clients in India. But I also lost somebody who had, in that process, become a close, much-valued friend.

That reinforces what I have stated earlier about how much disagreement between persons of different ethnic backgrounds and/or from different countries likely will always make us realize how much we all have in common when we get to know each other better and why we thus should cooperate instead of often fighting each other. Something which I have been richly blessed to see also happening related to many other colleagues or co-workers worldwide, plus with clients as well, all of whom I have been so fortunate to work and serve together with over the years in many different countries.

CHAPTER 22

TRANSITIONS AND STAYING RELEVANT

A mong the numerous important things I have learned from having been in charge of Msaada Architects for about four decades was the necessity to continue being relevant and ready to provide what is needed in the developing world, as many things naturally change. This underscores, therefore, also why the just mentioned capacity building is so crucially important. However, to also be faithful to Msaada Architects' original vision of responding to true needs for building projects in the developing world by specifically Christian churches, missions, and related organizations, we have, as mentioned before, often gone well beyond addressing brick-and-mortar issues.

When I co-founded Msaada Architects together with two passive partners in 1980, I had already realized a true need for also serving beyond Tanzania. So, after working/serving a bit more than one year in Nigeria, followed by six years in Tanzania, the need for what became Msaada Architects seemed, thus, eventually obvious to me, although I at that time had certainly not expected it to become my lifelong vocation.

Msaada Architects' Initial Transitions
During Msaada Architects' initial about 40-year history, there was always a definite need to adjust to changed realities in the developing

world. A notable example of this was when our Tanzania office started to measure quantities of materials needed for projects and to assist with importing what was not locally available from neighboring Kenya and, if so required, from the Western world.

Another major transition that required much serious rethinking was based on a totally unexpected situation, which, as mentioned often, arose when, at the turn of the last millennium, Msaada Architects was serving mostly on projects that had funding coming from Europe. For when all the church-related organizations providing that funding changed from funding many brick-and-mortar projects to focusing instead on funding programs, we could have decided to "close shop" at Msaada Architects.

That did not seem to be the right solution, though, since there still was — and is — a great need for more financial equity between the Western and the developing parts of the world. And that in a situation where the Western world amounts to only about 1/8 of the world's population but still has by far most of its wealth. Thus, it seemed churches in the developing world still needed Msaada if some of their projects were to materialize.

Msaada Architects therefore decided to help also by creating something that could replace even just a minuscule part of the funding that was no longer coming from Europe with funding from the U.S. which we took initiative to hopefully help provide. That resulted in the three earlier mentioned programs for financial support of projects in the developing world, which used Msaada's 501©3 status to provide some funding for these projects. But we have had mixed success with those programs largely because making them work efficiently requires much effort related to non-traditional A/E services, which is more complicated for an A/E nonprofit organization to bill clients for.

I still appreciate, though, how the decision was made around the year 2000 that Msaada Architects should continue to serve based on its original vision. However, had I known in advance how tough that transition would be financially, I might likely not have done so, although we then had 30+ staff members working in our home office in Minnesota or in the Africa area offices. This transition also occurred when most of the projects our associate office in India was working on were those done in association with Msaada.

So, fortunately the decision was made not to close the organization, although we did close our Africa area offices and replaced them with associate offices. And while we did not lay off any staff in the Minnesota home office, this decision put my wife and me in an extremely tight financial situation. For I have always felt — maybe wrongly, many have suggested to me — a personal responsibility to ensure Msaada could continue to work and operate based entirely (or almost so) on fees received for services provided.

It was, therefore, fortunate that the pastors in my Lutheran home congregation in Minnesota at that time connected me with two successful businesspersons who were ready to temporarily support projects in the developing world and for a short period to also help cover Msaada's operating expenses. Requiring the latter, fortunately, did not last long and, eventually, our staff was reduced by some employees retiring from the home office and us starting to work with associate offices in Africa, as we already had done so successfully in India.

One of the two people from my congregation who assisted us financially during that tough transition was Mark Johnson. The following is an excerpt from a letter the organization received from Mark, after he had been to India and seen some of the projects Msaada had been instrumental in making happen: **"If I had really known what God had in store for me when I first learned about MSAADA, I probably wouldn't have agreed to help. Like any great commitment we make in life, this one didn't come with an operating manual, although it did come with a sponsor: God. This time, God knew I needed a teacher, a mentor, a 'guide' beside me. God picked Poul Bertelsen for this, and what a teacher he has been!"**

Mark made a trip to India with four other men to primarily spend time visiting projects where Msaada had been the A/E. He also agreed to be chair of the organization's board. I will always be grateful for having learned so much from him, especially related to how financial matters are best dealt with in the U.S.

Further, because of Mark, I was fortunate to also be introduced to his friend and partner in some business ventures, Mike Ayres, who also had been on the trip to India together with Mark and three other men. This led Mike to also start supporting Msaada during the transition around the year 2000. Later, Mike succeeded Mark as chair of our board, and I am, similarly, extremely grateful for all I have learned from working and serving together with Mike for several years.

I better clarify though how I am not referring to Msaada Architects' transitions in order to suggest that is how things always should be done when providing services in the developing world, for we also have made many mistakes. And as mentioned already, I have maybe been too willing to take personal responsibility for things — also financially — that I maybe should not have taken. Although I was doing so with the intentions to ensure that our efforts resulted in Msaada's and my own main objective being met, namely that as many projects as possible would be happening for the benefit of enhancing the lives of our global neighbors!

Because of that, I have thus also always tried to stay focused on making personal decisions about Msaada Architects from a concern of it truly being able to serve churches and missions with their building projects in that part of the world more than by giving too much consideration for how it might be easiest and most convenient to do so from the Western world, including also for me personally as the Executive Director.

And since the local churches in the developing world — which uses Msaada Architects' services — almost always deal with tight financial situations around their activities and outreach to their communities, it seemed to me, that we shouldn't be too different from them to have at least some sense of solidarity with the churches we have been so blessed to serve overseas. Although it is hard to truly believe you do so when comparing what you are doing to what Christians in the developing world are often expected to deal with.

So, it has always, for me, been as mentioned more important for Msaada to ensure that as many as possible, viable and needed projects materialized than for our organization to avoid its own financial challenges. Something which has also taught us to be more trusting in God, providing financially for what we have been doing. That is, as mentioned often, also what churches in the developing world usually always must do, with more trust and faith in God providing what is needed than we often have in the Western World.

Msaada's Leadership Transition

Another major transition during Msaada's now 40+-year history was the transition not too long ago, when I passed on the position of Executive Director, so that I instead became a general consultant to be involved only as might be needed or required. The process of planning for that to happen commenced already in 2012, but it did not happen until at the turn of the years 2019 to 2020.

It has been a transition, though, which became more complicated than expected, being it coincided with the global spread of COVID-19. This has meant fewer possibilities for traveling overseas, and that has also made the transition more complicated for my immediate successor, after many clients have delayed and, in some cases, even canceled projects that were already planned in the developing world. But it is positive how it again is easier to travel overseas for all indications seem to be that there still is a need in the developing world for services like those Msaada provides, with especially many of those involving non- traditional A/E services.

However, in addition to making changes related to how the organization operates financially, my immediate successor as Executive Director has further been researching how truly needed the organization still is as well as where it is most needed. And with W. Jerry Murray being only a dozen years younger than me, there was also a need in the not-too-distant future for him to pass on the leadership of Msaada Architects to somebody younger. Something which has led to the announcement recently that Andrew Ripp will be executive director staring January 1, 2025.

Thus, as aforementioned, some changes have already been implemented related to how Msaada operates. But it is somehow disappointing that the organization now seems to have chosen to operate more like other American A/E organizations presently being involved in the developing world. So, while my successor as Executive Director has felt it was necessary to make this change, it should be of some concern, I believe, if the organization stops breaking new ground in the developing world. For in the past, we did this based always on determining how Western world nonprofit architects and engineers can most effectively and least expensively serve on church-sponsored projects in the developing world. This was all done to help assist in creating more financial equality in and with that part of the world, even when that meant providing non-traditional services beyond what A/Es usually do.

Alternatively, if there at some time no longer might be a need in the developing world for serving as Msaada has done earlier, as a nonprofit organization providing quality A/E services for the lowest possible fees, maybe there instead might be a need to assist church sponsored building projects here in the U.S., where presently many denominations and their congregations have a changing need regarding physical facilities.

A need which is not like when Msaada earlier served on a few U S. building projects for congregations requiring additional spaces. Instead, many U.S. congregations now have the opposite need instead regarding how to best utilize excess spaces in a relevant good stewardship way. Meeting such a need might also keep Msaada still as being groundbreaking in ways of serving appropriately the worldwide Body of Christ as a non-profit A/E organization.

Returning to the changes already made in Msaada — primarily to ensure better financial sustainability — I appreciate how that task became my successor's responsibility. For such changes would have been difficult for me to carry out, as I continued for four decades to work and serve based on what I, as a Scandinavian, still believe in and have learned from growing up in one of the Nordic countries, where I continue to believe the best of capitalism and the best of socialism have been mixed rather successfully with Christianity and its values being one of the pillars behind that. Something which has even resulted in those countries still having very high living standards despite them recently also having been called **"social investment countries"** as I have mentioned earlier.

Related to the rather diffuse term "human happiness" which has often been used with reference to the population of the Nordic countries, I have found personally, how happiness for me has meant finding meaning and joy in relationship with others and in doing what I feel now is a vocation for me. That has also meant meeting challenges related to that by living with gratitude to our God and creator for this earth of ours as well as for life generally.

Contrary to that, I have come to believe that many wealthy individuals in this country have fallen victim to what I have come to think of as the **"curse of greed."** I must admit, though, how that phenomenon is now also becoming more common in Europe, including in the Nordic countries. Thus, many persons in those countries have become concerned about whether the most often called **"welfare countries"** might eventually collapse and be replaced with a situation more like here in the U.S. with focus on everybody being expected to primarily take care of themselves, instead of ensuring more equality for all a country's citizens.

I would consider such a development an unfortunate setback, for the five Nordic countries, would likely result in higher consumerism also, all which will probably not result in happier populations, after the Nordic countries for some years now have supposedly had the happiest populations in the world. And that despite the rather high taxes in those countries to ensure more equality so everybody can jointly state, **"we**

all do better when we all do better!" That is an anonymous quote which I first saw at the Danish small island of Aeroe and something I believe should also be strived for globally.

And while I am aware how many Americans believe—wrongly, I think based also on recent political developments in the U.S.—that only capitalism provides prosperity for all. Thus, let me reiterate how I believe the right mixture of the best of capitalism and the best of socialism might better guarantee success globally as well.

N, F. S. Grundtvig

I should add to that though, how I recall the earlier mentioned 19th century Danish pastor, educator and hymn writer, having supposedly said something like "we are all healthier when we are all heathier and we are all richer when we are all richer". So, although this book is primarily about responsive architecture, it seems relevant to include further reference to a Danish important historical figure, who has influenced me to end up with the very meaningful career I have had as an architect.

This might then include how Grundtvig is quoted as having said — as referred to earlier — how we should emphasize humanity before religion, and that we as Christians should aim at societies "**where only a few have too much and even fewer too little.**" That also relates to what I learned relatively early in my adult life — after accepting the call to go to Nigeria — that we all must be aware there are others in this world than ourselves, and that every human life is equally important. That also relates to what has been said with justification related to climate change: how we should learn from nature, which has the importance of humility as its most important lesson for us humans.

That is an attitude which will also help us realize the unfortunate truth of what I read a person expressing once, namely that what we often label "development" also means unfortunately that "**while we humans earlier loved people and used things we now often love things and use people**". The result has been in my opinion a too excessive materialism and disproportionate individualism without enough regard for others.

Thus, there are now, unfortunately, many people in the Nordic countries also who apparently believe that the welfare states are like what in the Scandinavian languages is called a "smoergaasbord" to eat from, where everybody can take whatever, they desire or personally feel entitled to get. This was never the intention of the welfare programs, which instead are to be a kind of an insurance for that all a country's citizens can jointly have a better life.

So getting back to Grundtvig, who has so greatly inspired many in the Nordic countries — even to the extent that he is recognized as having helped make these countries what they are today. But while Grundtvig has never been recognized internationally, as have his contemporary middle of the 19th century well known Danes as Soeren, Kierkegaard and Hans Christiaan Andersen that seems to have changed a bit in recent years.

I have, for example, noted how there in 2018 was a symposium at the University of London on the international influence of Grundtvig from the "Lands of the Living," with 50 participants from 14 different countries. The influence of Grundtvig's groundbreaking principles was summarized into four brief ones: Cherish Life, Cherish Nature, Cherish People (especially ordinary people) and Cherish Lifelong Learning.

That all relates to how politics in the Scandinavian – or Nordic – countries have so far continued to be based largely on Christian values and those countries' educational systems. For Grundtvig was also the originator of the **Folk School Movement**, which has long been popular in those countries supporting lifelong learning. This involves how students usually don't sit for exams in folk schools, and they aren't graded either for what has been learned, but simply being recognized for having attended a folk school thus supporting the basic idea of simply learning for the sake of learning.

This is an idea that, in recent years, has been tried out by many other countries in Europe, Asia, and Africa, as well as in the U.S. That is mostly known here due to the **Highlander Folk School Movement**, which, in President Obama's speech at a dinner at the White House for the 5 Nordic Prime Ministers on May 13, 2016, had as its major theme how that educational idea by Grundtvig influenced also the 1960s Civil Rights Movement in the U.S. That was after many of its leaders had attended the Highlander Folk School, including Ralph Abernathy, John Lewis, and not least Dr. Martin Luther King Jr. Further so I have understood did also, for example, Rosa Parks.

Before closing regarding Grundtvig, let me add, how he was interested in more than "book learning" for everybody, as he also stressed the integrity of working with one's own hands. Related to that, I personally have in numerous ways benefited greatly from me having worked as a bricklayer's apprentice in the process of becoming an architect.

Grundtvig also stressed how lifelong learning and education are necessary for democracy to survive and thrive. Something which it is important to be reminded about also in this still rather new twenty-first century, so many years after Grundtvig presented his still relevant ideas and concerns related to faith, religion, education and politics.

He also suggested that being truthful requires humanity to be linked to the divine through "The Living Word" from God, which — as I understand his opinion — even preceded the Bible and the use of that. This is all something which I also see as part of what I have tried my best to do through what became my lifelong vocation, serving as a Master Builder in primarily the developing world.

Being True to the Past While Staying Relevant
I believe it is important to stay true to the past. But what is at any time required should be continually evaluated in addition to when and where it is required. This is valid also in the developing world and, therefore, is important to consider also for Msaada Architects.

However, all planning earlier related to the future of Msaada has also been based on the serious concern for that it would seem extremely unfortunate if the extensive A/E experiences that the organization has had for now over four decades dealing with building projects in the developing world would be lost and thus might no longer be available for primarily church-sponsored projects in primarily the developing world.

So, this book will hopefully also assist in preventing that from happening. In relation to Msaada Architects of the future, I also recognize how more changes are likely needed for it to remain relevant in a different world today from when the organization was founded in 1980. So, I wish my successors and their co-workers all the best as they continue to serve in the developing world. And I have in the past noted how serious adjustments for reasons we have had little control over have been required at least about every two decades.

There will, though, hopefully also be a time soon when A/E organizations like Msaada can simply compete equally with local A/E firms from the developing world, with all providing services that help ensure churches and related organizations will continue to get the best possible value for their money, and, thus, also the best possible facilities for providing improved services for our global neighbors, who depend so much on the services to be provided in these new facilities for them to truly enhance their lives.

And although the COVID-19 pandemic has resulted in so much illness and so many deaths, it has also made us realize how much smaller the world can be or might feel if we also use hybrid and virtual opportunities to collaborate. This can then also reduce air travel, which can help in reducing global warming. It is also for that reason important that Msaada Architects continues to adjust as required for serving in the developing world.

It is further important that all architects and engineers who work in the developing world are ready to provide quality services for reasonable financial compensation to enable much-needed projects to materialize. But based on my experiences now from over five decades having been involved with building projects in the developing world, let me reiterate how I believe **church-sponsored building projects benefits**

when involved architects and/or building engineers serve as master builders, whether they are from the Western world or whether they are local building professionals.

Appreciation and Thanksgiving

Finally, I understand how the Msaada of the future will be somehow different from Msaada of the past. And being a U.S. organization; it thus should likely also be organized financially more like competitive organizations now serving on a nonprofit basis in the developing world. I am, though, thankful the organization operated financially as it did originally until when I retired as the executive director.

I am also thankful that Msaada has allowed me the opportunity to follow my bliss — as I have heard it expressed so well — so in a meaningful way I have been able to do something in my life, which I truly have appreciated and enjoyed. Because although I would never have been able to be the best in anything specific, I have been able to utilize how God has given me a variety of skills, which I could use to hopefully have benefitted those whose lives have been enhanced through the services provided in the numerous physical facilities Msaada has been involved with as a Master Builder.

I must importantly add, though, how that would not have been possible without the emotional and other support I have always had from my wife Susanna related to Msaada Architects. Something for which I am eternally thankful. Without her ever having been directly involved in the organization daily, she has always wholeheartedly supported what I have been richly blessed to be involved with through that organization.

Susanna, therefore, has always shared in the excitement about what amazing effect has come from the many projects having been implemented in so many countries worldwide through the involvement of Msaada, so those physical facilities can be used to provide much-needed life-enhancing services for our global neighbors. My thanks for that thus goes to Susanna but also to Kennet, Marian, and Nathan — our three grown children now with their own families — whom we have been richly blessed to be the parents of and now also grandparents for their children.

Those sincere thanks of mine also include appreciation for how Susanna always has been more than ready to have had numerous friends and co-workers — whom I have been fortunate to serve with overseas — stay with us in our private home when they have visited the Twin Cities. And thanks also to her and to our three children, for how they have accepted me, having been away from home for project-related travel as extensively as I was for so long serving in many other parts of, especially, the developing world.

In closing, I want to add, as I also did in *Design & Dignity*, that **to God be the glory** for what we in Msaada Architects and what I, personally, have been richly blessed to see implemented of church-sponsored building projects in the developing world. As human beings, we can serve our great triune God only as "tools or instruments" in whatever role we who hope to "qualify" as being true followers of Jesus the Christ might have been allowed to play in the "Great Commission."

Chronology of the Initial Four Decades of Msaada Architects

1979: Poul Bertelsen came to Minnesota after having served six years as a Danish Mission Society (DMS) missionary architect in Tanzania. While in Arusha, Poul turned an existing building department — which earlier had been doing mainly maintenance of existing properties of the Evangelical Lutheran Church in Tanzanua (ELCT) — into an architectural and engineering department located in the national office of that church. After co-founding Msaada Architects in Minnesota — with logistical and financial assistance from David Simonson and Art Vikse — Poul was named executive director of this nonprofit architectural & engineering service organization and related to that, he was thus also invited to become a DMS associate missionary.

1980: Msaada Architects was officially incorporated in Minnesota. Its first project was a renovation and extension of Makiungu Hospital in Tanzania for the Medical Missionaries of Mary, with the project being funded by Misereor in Germany. Later that year, Msaada opened its first overseas area office in Arusha, Tanzania, after a large project for Bunda College of National Education — with funding from the EZE in Germany — was to be done for Tanzania Mennonite Church. W. Jerry Murray, who had worked part-time in the Minnesota home office, became late that year the first resident architect in charge of that initial area office. This was also the year when architect Herman Wagner started working for Msaada from his home in Germany and structural engineer Niels Graulund did the same from Denmark. Both Herman and Niels had earlier experiences from serving churches on building projects in Tanzania.

1982: Msaada opened a second Africa area office now in Antananarivo, Madagascar, after receiving a request to do so from the Malagasy Lutheran Church (FLM) and the American Lutheran Church (ALC) with the latter then being headquartered in Minneapolis, Minnesota. The office in Antananarivo functioned almost as a department of the FLM, and the first resident architect in charge was Peter Ozolins. Later that year, Douglas Hincks became the first resident civil/structural engineer in the Arusha, Tanzania, area office.

1983: Msaada was asked by the Arcot Lutheran Church and the DMS to be the architect of what grew to be a very large school project in India. An associate office arrangement was eventually made early in 1986 with J. Inbaraaj Consultants, after Msaada had unsuccessfully tried an association with another Indian architect. Prior to that, a project was done in Pakistan, and a few projects were later done in Bangladesh.

1984: Msaada opened a third Africa area office, which also was to be a regional Africa office this time in Nairobi, Kenya. That was after the organization had become increasingly involved with projects in several African countries outside Tanzania. W. Jerry Murray moved from the Arusha office to be the initial resident architect in charge of the Nairobi office, while Douglas Hinck took charge of the Arusha office. This was also the year when DanChurchAid took over the responsibility from the DMS as the Danish church related organization dealing on behalf of the Danish governmental aid organization (DANIDA) with the Arcot Lutheran Church for what became the large ALC School Project. A relationship which for Msaada resulted in getting further involved in India outside also of that large project.

1986: Peter Ozolins moved to the Arusha office to assist there and Scott Williams became the second resident architect in charge of the Antananarivo office. After Msaada initially was asked to serve on projects funded in Tanzania, Madagascar and other African countries by the Lutheran World Foundation (LWF), this led to serving on LWF funded projects in India, also with a notable one being the large Gossner College project.

1988: Msaada was recognized as a related organization by the newly established Evangelical Lutheran Church in America (ELCA) through the Division for Global Mission having a representative on Msaada's board.

1990: That was a year of many changes as both W. jerry Murray and Douglas Hincks left Msaada and returned to their home countries in the USA and Canada, after they each had spent about 8 years in East Africa. Scott Williams returned to the Minnesota office to be studio chief architect after he had spent 3+ years in first the Antananarivo office and later in the Nairobi office. The following years as well as the previous decade saw further the following as expat resident architects or engineers in the Nairobi and Arusha offices: Douglas Francis, Verle Hansen, Andrew Greeley, Matthew Carlquist, Terry Peach, John Kraft, Jeffrey Benson, William Lycett and Henning Dammeyer. During the same period Charles Whelan, Loren Morschen and Royce Wiens followed each other as the resident architect in the Antananarivo office and Philip Burdick was for about a year resident architect in a new area office in Addis Abeba, Ethiopia, while an otherwise retired architect Richard Blundell for a few years served on a volunteer basis as Msaada's representative in Cameroon.

1992: That was a different year largely due to a most unfortunate and terrible reason, as that was when Timothy Olson went to Bangui in the Central African Republic to be Clerk of Works for a new Lutheran church to be built there. He also functioned somehow as the building contractor for the construction work. However, Tim was brutally killed by bandits when he had gone for vacation in a part of the country where foreigners were strongly advised against visiting. Like by a miracle another young Minnesotan, Tim Dray, stepped forward to go to Bangui to complete the project, and later the so unfortunate death of Tim Olson led to the founding of Lutheran Partners in Global Ministry (LPGM), being also the organization with which Msaada later shared our initial office space in the Minnesota Church Center in Minneapolis, after the office earlier had been in Wayzata and Deephaven plus near the U of M campus in Minneapolis.

1995: Msaada initiated its first project in the United States when we were literally "ordered" by the Medical Missionaries of Mary to do an extension of their house in Boston, MA. By the mid-nineties there were already a sizeable number of young architectural graduates, who had served in the Minnesota home office, besides those who later went on to be resident architects in the African area offices. Without no longer recalling nearly all of them, it is maybe not fair to mention just a few. But they did include Jack Amdal, Ellen Luken, Ben Black, Carl Robertson, Sandra Mallory, Scott Lundberg, Jason Krumm, Elizabeth Forslund, Patricia Mestenhauser Berg, with the latter also being stationed in Cameroon for a year. Peter Kramer assisted periodically with design work as a very creative architect, and so did Mario Anschutz from Germany and Ildze Alaya from Colombia each for several months. Arthur W. Peabody was a part-time experienced architect who also was a structural engineer, and he functioned as such on numerous projects. Structural engineering was also dealt with by the local engineers in the area or associate offices. When Arthur Peabody retired, Msaada was pleased to arrange for structural engineering services with Bernie Stroh of Stroh Engineering. Something which worked exceedingly well for many years, even after that firm moved from Minneapolis to Hawaii. Capable clerical staff in the Minnesota office included up until and through that time: Deana Miller, Delores Scherling, Marian Kyllo, Beverly Meakins, Khin Black and Kathy Kenny.

1997: The significant decrease in projects being funded by European donor organizations for churches and missions in the developing world began at the end of that year. A couple of years later resulted in those organizations almost overnight dropping supporting bricks and mortar projects in favor of supporting programs instead. Until that time, these organizations had funded partly or fully most of the projects with which Msaada had been involved. Thus, a transition for Msaada was initiated to try to replace European-sponsored project funding with at least some projects sponsored by U.S.-based organizations. A tithing program was thus also initiated by Msaada, which was later named Sharing the Blessings when Lutheran Partners in Global Ministry joined in promoting that program.

1998: Msaada did a first project in Latvia, which began a sizeable project involvement not only in the three Baltic countries but also in mostly other independent countries that earlier had been part of the Soviet Union as well as in Russia itself. That involvement was initially centered on the Lutheran Church Missouri Synod (LCMS), World Mission supported projects and it included doing projects in for example Kazakhstan, Kyrgyzstan, and Armenia, but also in other developing countries such as the Philippines, Mexico, Jamaica and South Africa as well as a few European projects in Greece, England, and Germany.

1999: Msaada began doing a few church projects in the USA, after Our Savior Lutheran Church in Faulkton, South Dakota asked for design of a new church. That was accepted due to the decisions by European church related donors to support bricks and mortar projects no longer primarily in Africa, India and other parts of the developing world.

2001: Msaada discontinued operating its own offices in Arusha and Nairobi and instead initiated associate arrangements with indigenous architects and engineers. For projects in Tanzania, Msaada first associated with Triple A in Arusha and later with ITECO Consult Tanzania in

Morogoro. Ultimate Design in Nairobi became Msaada's associate in Kenya. Primarily the office in Arusha had before that for years a strong local staff headed up by architect Joas Tibaijuka, engineer Aziz Moshi and clerk of works E. O. Mwambo.

2004: The office in Antananarivo, Madagascar, became an independent office when, instead of Msaada seeking an associate relationship with another indigenous firm, the staff asked to carry on independently with the existing office as kind of an Msaada franchise and thus retaining locally the well-known name Msaada Madagascar. Jacquelin Randrianirina was, for the years of that office, the key local staff person.

2005: Msaada Architects celebrated twenty-five years of service on church-sponsored building projects worldwide, with not only numerous projects having been implemented but also with many more for which Msaada had provided initial planning and design services without them yet having been funded.

2007: It seemed now apparent that in order for Msaada to continue to truly serve the needs of church-sponsored building projects in the developing world, services should maybe be expanded to also be more of a development facilitator. That, therefore, also involved helping locate funding for at least the initial part of worthy building projects. But with new requests from countries worldwide for architectural and engineering services as Msaada had provided since it was founded in 1980, it became difficult to follow up on the role as a development facilitator. Further an unsuccessful attempt to have on staff a fundraiser delayed implementation of this new strategy. Instead, Msaada resumed its earlier busier original role as primarily being architect/engineer. The main difference was that most projects in the twenty-first century have been funded from the United States as opposed to the period of 1980-2000 when by far the most projects which Msaada was involved with in the developing world had European funding.

2010: After having felt the worldwide recession, Msaada was able to again get back to a stronger and steady workload that included following up on projects where we had served before — mostly in Africa and India — as well as new projects in for example Colombia and Haiti, with the latter needing to rebuild after a large devastating earthquake that year. That was also the year when Poul Bertelsen started what ended up being for almost a decade teaching annually a half spring semester graduate class at the School of Architecture at the University of Minnesota. It was also when a young architectural graduate, Jeffrey Potts, went to Uganda for a bit more than a year to be Msaada's representative on projects there.

2011: The positive trend continued, with Msaada becoming increasingly involved again in African countries, but especially in Liberia, which was rebuilding after a civil war. So, Anne Hake, Peter Leaky and Russ Anderon were located as staff or a volunteer in Monrovia, Liberia, for shorter periods. Further involvement also included after the earthquake in Haiti to begin establishing an area office in Port-au-Prince, Haiti with Andrew Ripp as the resident architect. Getting involved with many Haiti projects meant a requirement on some projects with U.S. funding to have mechanical and electric designs done by a U: S. certified firm. Thus, a successful arrangement was made with M and E Engineering regarding that. Periodic requirement of a civil engineer in some design work was usually met by Kennet Bertelsen, while Brian Dobie was utilized as an extremely experienced Geotech engineer.

2013: After Poul Bertelsen, in late 2012, had turned 70 years old, plans began for the organization's transition to somebody else being in charge. That was suggested to ideally last only 3 or max 5 years. It was to focus on how best to ensure that Msaada could continue using its extensive experiences in serving primarily the needs of church-sponsored building projects in the developing world.

2014: Msaada opened again an office in Tanzania — this time in Mwanza — based on a request to serve mostly in that area of the country on medical projects funded by the New York based Touch Foundation. Initially, Peter Leaky and later John Wade went to Tanzania for that. And while there also had been an increasing involvement in projects in other African countries, where Msaada earlier had been extensively involved, South Sudan was among the countries now added to those being served. Further, Msaada was blessed to seeing numerous projects implemented in Haiti with the largest being rebuilt after the 2010 earthquake, a 250-bed teaching hospital related to Notre Dame University in Haiti.

2017: This became a critical year as the Tanzania office was closed by mid-year, after a good deal of projects in the Mwanza area had been completed. Further projects now became extra complicated to do in some countries because of civil unrest in primarily the English-speaking part of Cameroon as well as in South Sudan. As mentioned earlier related to staff in the Minnesota home office it is maybe unwise to try to mention just a few of the design staff after year 2000, but they included Alyssa Jagdfeld, Tim Helmeke, Caius Momanyi, James Nestingen, Jacob Wollensak, Beth Evanson, Rocio Munez and again Jason Krumm, while clerical staff included Deb Ringblom, Erica Boyles, Marian Bradburn and Shirley Bolstad. Preparing this chronology has further exposed the interesting fact that it seems over the years more than hundred staff members have hopefully been positively inspired from having served in the Msaada Architects' home office in Minnesota. That is, in addition to local staff in the Africa area, offices as well as staff in the overseas associate offices.

2018: When Poul Bertelsen and his wife Susanna went to Ohio for something else, they used the opportunity to also visit Jerry Murray and his wife Sue. Conversations with them ended up including the future of Msaada, and Jerry therefore offered to lend some assistance in defining the future direction for the organization. That seemed to be divine inter-vention, as he later confirmed an interest in becoming Exec Dir of Msaada. Further, by year end, Andrew Ripp resigned from Msaada after having seen over 80 projects implemented in Haiti, while completed and implemented projects by Msaada worldwide had now reached over 900.

2019: The year begun with Euvodine Exantus-Jean as architect in charge of Msaada Haiti, after she had been on staff locally for as few years. It also became a year with major transitions, after Jerry Murray accelerated resigning from his local private firm to become Msaada's Exec Dir just before the year end, and after him having worked as a part-time volunteer development director. Poul Bertelsen likewise worked as a volunteer for the second half of the year, as there was a significant reduction in new larger projects. It was thus due to logistical reasons also decided to move the home office to Findlay, Ohio, where Jerry Murray already resided, and the organization's name was officially changed to be Msaada Architects from MSAADA Architects.

2020: The year started with the home office being in Ohio, and with Poul Bertelsen and Scott Williams designated as general consultant and design consultant working out of Minneapolis. So, the ministry contin-ued, but at a new location. The changes were also based on an expecta-tion that fee income might need to be supplemented with grants and/or donations. That was partly because of the slowdown in project activity, which worsened significantly after the pandemic hit the whole world, and thus with many already planned projects in the developing world being delayed or even cancelled. That meant for Msaada that also, for example, a large planned new hospital project in Malawi was cancelled by the donor after preliminary planning and design had successfully been completed. Such project developments plus the pandemic were also why earlier plans for celebrating that year the 40th anniversary of Msaada Architects were initially postponed and later cancelled.

www.ingramcontent.com/pod-product-compliance
Lightning Source LLC
Chambersburg PA
CBHW070909120626
46546CB00001B/194